COSTING LABOR CONTRACTS AND JUDGING THEIR FINANCIAL IMPACT

Stephen J. Holoviak

PRAEGER

PRAEGER SPECIAL STUDIES • PRAEGER SCIENTIFIC

New York • Philadelphia • Eastbourne, UK
Toronto • Hong Kong • Tokyo • Sydney

Library of Congress Cataloging in Publication Data

Holoviak, Stephen J.
Costing labor contracts and judging their financial impact.

Bibliography: p.
Includes index.
1. Employee fringe benefits—Costs. 2. Labor costs. 3. Wages. 4. Collective labor agreements. I. Title.
HD4928.N6H65 1984 658.1'553 84-15880
ISBN 0-03-071467-2 (alk. paper)

Published in 1984 by Praeger Publishers
CBS Educational and Professional Publishing
a Division of CBS Inc.
521 Fifth Avenue, New York, NY 10175 USA

456789 052 987654321

Printed in the United States of America
on acid-free paper

Acknowledgments

The decision to write this book resulted from conversations with both practitioners and teachers in the field of contract negotiations.

Practitioners, including labor union members/officials and company officials, expressed concern about their ability to assess the cost and impact of contract proposals accurately and completely. In addition, teachers perceived a lack of materials needed for teaching labor/personnel specialists how to cost contract proposals and how to judge the impact of those proposals on all aspects of company operations.

Once the need for this book was identified and the decision made to write it, those same practitioners, teachers, and also people in disciplines outside labor relations, made many valuable contributions to my work. Individuals with whom I spoke identified specific information regarding their personal strengths and weaknesses in calculating costs and impacts of contract proposals. In addition, I was able to gain insight into the levels of competency a person handling the contract-negotiating responsibility should ideally possess in order to make sound contract decisions in such areas as financial ratio analysis and accounting.

I wish to thank practitioners from both unions and companies for their input regarding how they handle financial aspects of negotiating, for their assistance in identifying ideal levels of competency in certain areas, and for their review and criticism of the material as the project unfolded.

I also appreciated review by knowledgeable practitioners of accounting, including Robert G. Baldassari, CPA, of the Washington, D.C., firm of Berlin, Seguin, Karan, and Ramos, who offered substantive help and advice in his review of material to insure accuracy and consistency; and Dr. Randyl Elkin, Director of Graduate Labor Studies at West Virginia University, for his helpful comments and review.

I wish to thank Susan Stone for her invaluable help and skill in editing the book and for her helpful comments and contribution. In addition, I appreciate the contribution of Fred Smith for his help in locating references. Finally, thanks to Dr. Joseph Hunt, Dean of the College of Business, Shippensburg University, for providing typing and preparation support for the manuscript.

Table of Contents

List of Tables

Table

List of Exhibits

Exhibit

Exhibit

1

Where the Costing Process Currently Stands

INTRODUCTION

Current economic conditions, especially the combined effects of recession, inflation, and high interest rates, have magnified the importance of even the smallest benefit decisions made during collective bargaining negotiations—for both union and company negotiators and for the people they represent.

Changes in wage rates and productivity relative to principal trading nations of the United States have been a source of concern for both labor and management. Over the 18-year period from 1960 to 1978, hourly wage rates in the United States increased three times, while they increased 20 times in Japan, 12 times in West Germany, and seven times in France (Report of U.S. President 1980).

Productivity statistics are no more optimistic. While, according to data from the Council on Wage and Price Stability and the Bureau of Labor Statistics, the U.S. worker is still more productive than the worker in the United States' principal trading nations, these nations are increasing their productivity at a greater rate. Between 1972 and 1978, the U.S. worker's output rose approximately 12 percent; worker's output in the principal trading nations rose 30 percent over the same period.

In addition, management has had to confront the reality of rising benefit costs. The U.S. Chamber of Commerce reported a 388 percent increase in the cost of benefits over the 20-year period from 1955 to 1975. In many companies, the benefit package cost exceeds 30 percent of the total payroll cost (Henderson 1979), and is expected to account for as much as 50 percent before the mid 1990s.

Not only are the costs of benefits getting higher, but also the returns to companies for such outlays tend to be low. Employees usually place minimal value on these benefits, take them for granted, and do not consider them as incentives for increased productivity (Henderson 1979). Unfortunately, the problems and concerns that face labor and management have been compounded by the fact that companies and unions have both failed to perform in-depth cost analyses of the benefits package.

All of the above problems and concerns are brought to the negotiating table. In the past, much of the difficulty encountered in reaching effective agreements has stemmed from misunderstandings and misperceptions on the part of all involved. These are due, in large measure, to the failure of unions and companies to perform in-depth cost analyses of benefit packages. This failure results in an inability to develop and communicate accurate and reliable figures, which means labor and management cannot reach a mutual understanding of the value of the benefit package and its long-range economic effects on both parties.

It is essential that appropriate guidelines be established to refine skill levels of practitioners and students in the fields of labor relations and collective bargaining. These guidelines require an integration of accounting, financial analysis, and labor relations principles in order to be effective in meeting the increasingly complex needs of negotiators at the collective bargaining table. The objective of this book is to provide the practitioner with these necessary guidelines:

1. To identify effective accounting, financial, and collective bargaining skills;
2. To suggest a method for integrating and utilizing those skills to better serve contract-bargaining needs; and
3. To develop contract proposals that take into account relevant costs and the impact of the proposal on the operation as a whole.

MANAGEMENT ORGANIZATION FOR BARGAINING

Companies organize their personnel and labor relations functions in different ways. Areas of responsibility for personnel and labor relations differ. Some companies may place the responsibility for the labor relations function at the corporate vice-presidential level, while others place it at the middle management level.

A 1965 Conference Board Survey report indicated that the head of corporate personnel functions reported to the chairman or president in 65 percent of the cases, whereas a 1979 Conference Board report indicated that labor relations staff personnel were present in the following hierarchy levels: corporate, 92 percent; division, 59 percent; and plant, 68 percent (Freedman 1979).

Another report in 1977 shows that 39 percent of personnel services and 47 percent of industrial relations functions were handled at the corporate rather than at division or plant levels (Christenson, Vancil, and Marshall 1979). This corresponds to a 1980 study of managerial structure in the coal industry that placed the locus of labor functions at corporate level (Holoviak 1980).

The number of labor relations staff persons employed by companies is usually determined by the number of unionized employees. Figures vary widely; however, according to a Conference Board Survey of 601 firms, the average number of labor relations staff persons is 13.4, with the average ratio of one staff member per 200 to 400 union members. The lower end of the survey shows companies reporting only one staff member for more than 1,000 union members (Kochan 1980).

As students and practitioners of labor relations are aware, location in the hierarchy coupled with commensurate authority of the labor staff person is important. The individual's location can affect the overall quality and effectiveness of labor-management relations for the company. Theory notes that a staff person should be located as near the operating site as possible with authority to settle labor disputes or problems that arise. This individual could have line authority over this situation.

While much of the literature suggests collective bargaining ought to be decentralized, Kochan believes that it may, in fact, be highly centralized in terms of management structure (Kochan 1980). There is a significant body of literature devoted to the argument regarding centralized versus decentralized structure. Much recent data suggest that the decentralized model of authority can result in more productive operations and also indicates that, if the data offered by Kochan are correct, U.S. collective bargaining systems may not be constructed along the lines of the more efficient model.

The area of authority referred to here is not overall authority and responsibility for the labor relations function. It is, rather, at what level in the hierarchy the responsibility for costing labor agreements, developing wage and benefit packages, and negotiating agreements falls. According to Kochan, in 90 percent of the 688 companies surveyed in the study, responsibility for costing labor agreements rested with labor staff specialists; while in 70 to 80 percent of the companies, responsibility for developing wage and benefit packages rested with a labor staff specialist (Kochan 1980). Kochan goes on to report that responsibility may be vested in these individuals, but the final authority for the items is given to the labor staff by only 20 percent of the companies (Kochan 1980). This indicates that authority and responsibility may not be evenly balanced.

UNION ORGANIZATION FOR BARGAINING

Union structure for collective bargaining appears to be reactive in nature; that is, its structure seems to flow in response to how companies organize for collective bargaining. If the survey work by Kochan is correct (that is, key decision-making for companies is highly centralized), then the move to centralized bargaining structure by unions over the past 20 years can be more easily understood. In certain case studies, such as with the phone industry and with the General Electric Company, the union organization developed a centralized bargaining form to balance the power of the companies.

In theory, decision-making should be concentrated at the point of bargaining. This is not the case with either unions or companies. Yet the union negotiators are vested with authority to make key decisions only to the extent they feel the membership will support these decisions. If the preparation has been carefully worked out and the agreements are within the International Convention guidelines, then membership support is fairly certain. In cases where there has been a lack of contact between leaders from the international, the local, and the rank-and-file, or if the membership is dissatisfied with its leadership, ratification of the contract becomes less certain.

Responsibility for costing contract terms depends on the size of the local and the importance of the negotiation. Support may come from specialists, the international staff, or be delegated to the field representative.

Lack of support from the international staff or the field representative need not spell defeat for the local negotiator. The local can present a strong and professional showing at the bargaining table through using some basic costing techniques and other available resources. Subsequent chapters in this book will help to prepare the person in charge of negotiations to handle the task in a knowledgeable fashion.

In summary, it should be noted that while both companies and unions currently have centralized organizations for collective bargaining negotiations, they are moving toward more decentralized organization. Skills, responsibility, and authority are not necessarily found in any one person, much less the person doing the negotiating. Ideally, both union and company negotiators would have the necessary skills and authority to negotiate effectively, backed up by informed and integrated contract-costing preparation by support staffs at a more centralized level.

KEY PROBLEMS IN EXISTING NEGOTIATING PROCEDURES

One key problem in existing negotiating procedures is that the people in charge of negotiations fail to utilize fully the wide assortment of technically skilled help available to them (Granof 1973). Available help includes experts from the accounting, finance, compensation, personnel, and planning departments.

Another reason that contract costing and other financial and planning aspects of labor relations are relatively inefficient is that they often fail to get enough data to work with or fail to use the correct types of data. Often, the only information company negotiators request from the technically skilled groups is summary-type payroll data (Granof 1973). While most companies prepare long-range plans that indicate anticipated volume, price, and capital investment, cost calculations for contract preparations are primarily limited to historic data. This assumes the labor usage ratio of the past will remain the same in the future. However, other company operations are based on projections of future operations contained in long-range plans.

In addition, labor contract analysts and negotiators tend to disregard the effects of their decisions on other functional areas of company operations. This could be a result of limited information from other departments or of insufficient skills to complete the analysis.

ROLE OF COMPUTERS

With all the complexities involved in costing a labor contract, it is natural to assume that computers have been used extensively in the approximately 193,000 agreements that are in effect. In reality, few companies or unions have applied the sophisticated computer-aided mathematical techniques used elsewhere in organizations for costing anticipated union demands.

In a survey of 225 Fortune Directory Companies (Caples 1969), only seven report the use of programs specially designed for costing variables in the collective bargaining process. None report continued use during negotiations, either as a mathematical model or to test alternative union demands. Caples finished his analysis by stating that "the use of computers to prepare for bargaining is in its infancy—or possibly it is still in the fetal stage."

It appears the major use of computers in the bargaining process by both companies and unions is for running standard electronic data processing (EDP) reports, results of which are individually analyzed. Information ranging from grievance arbitration files to analysis of company economic profiles is gathered in the preparation stage on subjects.

The International Union Department (IUD) keeps on record 22 key contract provisions of 208 major contracts in both manufacturing and nonmanufacturing companies. While these data are helpful and do tend to ensure equitable demands across industries, the IUD programs do not attempt to model contract proposals or project the costs of union demands.

Union response in the Caples survey regarding problems encountered in using computers centered on the lack of useful data sources. Some companies commented that their unions used computers to develop, analyze, and defend certain demands. However, 56 percent report the union makes no use of computers in preparing for negotiations.

Any computer application for many of the problems encountered in the collective bargaining process is still theoretical. This is due to the loosely structured nature of labor relations problems. Yet computer application for costing contract demands is quite feasible.

Much of the problem in using computers rests with the fact that companies and unions fail to implement a comprehensive record-keeping system. For example, EDP records of data on absenteeism may record only the person's time away from the job. Yet, to record the cost properly, the record should include data regarding allowances for replacement personnel and any deviations in output resulting from the absenteeism of the more skilled person.

Use of computers is widely accepted in personnel areas, but the records kept need to be improved so they include a broader body of information. Future computer applications depend on adequate data bases from which to make complete cost analysis. For instance, various aspects of contracts explored in future chapters of this volume will include reference to "a total costing element," which involves costs of personnel processing, benefits for replacement workers, and so forth. This type of information represents the data collection necessary to build an effective data base for use in collective bargaining negotiations.

The potential for use of computers in collective bargaining is vast. Applications in the current state of the art are:

1. Analysis of past contract cost estimates to their actual cost;
2. Costing alternative package proposals during negotiations; and
3. Analyzing contract demands and their effect on wage rate, product price, productivity, and profit levels.

REVERSE COLLECTIVE BARGAINING

Reverse collective bargaining, or the concession of labor to management requests for "give backs" of wages or benefits agreed upon in previous contract negotiations, must be considered in any discussion of collective bargaining.

The goal of negotiations from the union perspective since the beginning of the labor movement in the 1930s has been to gain more for its constituency in terms of wages and benefits. Recently, however, labor has been willing to grant give backs to management if the company's ability to stay in business might be jeopardized by a disproportionate wage and benefit burden. Concessions can take the form of actual decreases in wages or benefits, wage or benefit freezes, sharply curtailed wage or benefit increases, or an end to restrictive work rules that reduce management's flexibility in assignment of workers.

An example of a positive reverse collective bargaining negotiation is the case of the Teamsters in 1981–82. They believed negotiations of this kind were needed to help the transportation industry. In fact, the Teamsters opened talks before the expiration of the existing agreements in the hope that they could help ailing truck companies with problems arising from industry deregulation.

Other industries that have recently utilized reverse collective bargaining include the airline, auto, rubber, and steel industries. The airline industry has experienced many changes since deregulation. Braniff, Continental, Eastern, Pan American, Republic, United, and Western have all been involved to some extent in trying to renegotiate contract provisions. Contract changes have centered on work rules to help increase productivity and to facilitate wage freezes and wage cuts. In late 1983 Continental and Eastern were involved in intensive renegotiation efforts that included the possibility of bankruptcy and reorganization of the companies.

Continental did, in fact, go into reorganization, which is a drastic step when one considers the ramifications of such a move. Continental's action left thousands of business travelers stranded around the country, which is bound to have long-term effects in marketing areas. In addition, Continental was perceived as using the reorganization as a means of voiding existing labor agreements. The long-term effects of this action will be watched closely by industry practitioners and researchers.

Auto industry renegotiations have centered on work rule flexibility, wage cuts, and suspension of cost-of-living adjustments. Chrysler Corporation workers have the most celebrated cases in this area. Chrysler's reported profitability in mid 1983 and the revelation of its intention to repay bail-out loans ahead of schedule caused the United Auto Workers Union to make moves toward recapturing the previously granted concessions. There have been numerous management/labor confrontations since that time.

Rubber industry managers obtained work rule changes and some wage cuts at both tire and nontire plants after indicating that over 20 plant closings might become necessary without these concessions.

The steel industry, in trouble for some time, has been plagued by difficult renegotiations. Industry analysts are not sure if the $2 billion in concessions received by the "big seven" (U.S. Steel, Bethlehem, Jones & Laughlin, National, Inland, Republic, and Armco) will be enough to help some producers achieve profitable levels (Knezevich 1983). Three producers are close to seeking Chapter 11 bankruptcy status (Knezevich 1983). Bethlehem Steel's situation at its Sparrows Point plant in Baltimore, Maryland, is an example of the difficulties faced in this industry. Plant officials and industry analysts suggest that plant operations are inefficient and overly expensive. The company lacks capital to install more efficient and productive equipment. The debt level of the company is the highest among major producers, and company officials claim their bankers refuse to lend more money for capital investments without a reduction in labor costs (Jones and Branham 1983).

For union officials, accepting the Bethlehem plan would mean the immediate loss of 500 jobs plus wage and benefit cuts for remaining employees. This is in exchange for future job security and company investment in modern equipment. Laid-off workers do not see any future possibility of being recalled, and the workers on the job claim the company is just trying to maximize its profits from investment by getting rid of employees (Jones 1983). There has also been evidence that many major steel companies are actually using their capital to diversify rather than to update their plants. Union officials are confused and arguing among themselves, and company officials have given the word that without concessions plants will close.

While unions have generally resisted the reverse collective bargaining movement, there are hundreds of cases of concesssions granted in recent negotiations. It should be noted that the granting of concessions is not a phenomenon unique to this current economic period. The following are cases of reverse collective bargaining discussed by Peter Henle (1973):

1. The Aluminum Workers granted concessions to Aliva at Chillicothe, Ohio;
2. The Bakery Workers, Teamsters, and Retail Wholesale Workers granted concessions to the American Biscuit Company;
3. The International Union of Electricians granted concessions to General Motors' Frigidaire plant at Dayton, Ohio, and Sylvania at Batavia, New York;
4. The Printing Trades Union granted concessions to Standard Register at Dayton, Ohio;

5. The Rubber Workers granted concessions to Goodyear at Windsor, New York, and the Firestone and Goodyear plants at Akron, Ohio; and
6. The United Auto Workers granted concessions to Chrysler Corporation.

The reverse collective bargaining process is not only time-consuming but also highly sensitive. The process requires careful and comprehensive planning, an atmosphere of mutual good faith between labor and management, political savvy and understanding, and effective handling of the complex variables involved. Trouble areas that have arisen in this process include:

1. Subsequent actions taken on the part of management that jeopardize its credibility with labor; and
2. Politically difficult situations that arise in subsequent negotiations stemming from establishing precedents in seemingly similar, yet actually different, situations.

Actions by management that jeopardize its credibility with labor include: salary increases, bonuses, or other forms of excess paid to the managerial staff; situations in which the company experiences excess profits and makes no move to recognize the worker's contribution and sacrifice; and senior management taking the situation for granted and assuming that once they have used reverse collective bargaining, it will always be available.

An example of a situation in which management jeopardized its long-range negotiating position through actions subsequent to the give back agreement would be the negotiations between General Motors and the United Auto Workers. Shortly after the United Auto Workers ratified a new contract with GM that granted contract concessions, GM officials announced a new bonus plan raising executive compensation. This produced widespread anger among union members that made further changes in work rules at local plant negotiations difficult.

Politically difficult situations that arise in subsequent negotiations stemming from establishing precedents in seemingly similar yet actually different situations, might occur when a local union deals with several companies. In that case, the union may receive complaints that the concessions to one company place other companies at a competitive disadvantage. Another politically difficult situation arises when competing unions try to take over representation of the workers by claiming that the current union representative's having given concessions proves the weakness of the representative in serving its membership.

In summary, reverse collective bargaining can be an important tool for assuring that businesses survive and, therefore, workers' jobs are saved. However, it requires careful planning, negotiations based on mutual trust and actual needs, and responsible follow-through on the part of both labor and management. It should be noted that there are very few cases where only labor's concessions have been of help to the company in trouble. To salvage a troubled company requires concessions and cooperation from both labor and management.

SUMMARY

Chapter 1 has been designed to help the reader gain insight into the current status of collective bargaining in the United States.

There are two interdependent points of view that must be examined. Wages, representing labor's point of view, and productivity, representing management's point of view, are increasing at a slower rate in the United States than in its principal trading nations. It is not hard to understand, with that in mind, that benefit costs to management and benefit value to workers are becoming increasingly important concerns. It is essential, therefore, that the benefit sections of collective bargaining agreements be developed effectively, in both short- and long-term perspective.

To deal effectively with these issues, the practitioner should understand who is responsible for negotiations for both labor and management, how each group tends to be organized, and problems each group faces in preparing for and carrying out the negotiating process.

In addition, the practitioner should be aware of the existing usefulness of computers and their huge potential for use in collective bargaining negotiations.

Also included in Chapter 1 is a section on reverse collective bargaining, which, while certainly controversial, is being used in industry with increasing frequency.

The remaining chapters in this book set forth a practical approach for developing and costing collective bargaining agreements that are mutually beneficial for labor and management.

2

The Cost of Wage Requests

INTRODUCTION

Wages make up the largest part of the compensation package for most companies and must therefore be costed accurately. A 1979 Chamber of Commerce Survey reports that the average company pay breakdown, excluding benefits, included 93.7 percent for straight time, 3.6 percent for premium pay (overtime), 0.6 percent for holiday pay, 0.6 percent for shift differentials, 1.1 percent for incentive pay, and 0.4 percent for other items. The breakdown for average hourly earnings as a percent of payroll and average hourly earnings as cents per hour is shown by industry groups in Table 2.1.

Wage-Productivity Debate

A problem of some concern to negotiators on both sides of the table has been that wage increases have outstripped productivity gains in recent years. The rate of change in productivity has varied considerably among industries recently. The Bureau of Labor Statistics notes that during the period from 1975 to 1980, three-fourths of reporting industries showed lower gains in productivity than were recorded between 1947 and 1975 (BLS Bulletin 2128, 1982). Nonfarm business productivity increased at a rate of 2.4 percent per year from 1947 to 1975, while the annual growth rate from 1975 to 1980 was only 0.6 percent (Bureau of Labor Statistics 1982).

On the other hand, compensation paid to employees has displayed a different trend. Table 2.2 shows the recorded compensation increases from 1950 through 1975 indexed for 1967 = 100. In terms of unit labor costs, the increases in various industries have displayed a similar pattern.

For an even clearer picture of what has been happening, compensation trends can be compared with trends in output per man-hour. Indexed with 1967 = 100, and examining from that period to 1978, compensation has increased 8 percent per year between 1967 and 1978, while output has increased only 1.2 percent during the same period (see Table 2.3).

Are Unions to Blame for Productivity Declines and Spiraling Wages?

Union negotiators use the evidence of increased worker output as justification for demanding higher wages. Their rationale is that if productivity is increasing, there must certainly be new and higher profits available from which the wages demanded can be paid. The assumption by union negotiators is that all other factors involved in production have remained the same and the increased productivity has resulted from labor contributions only. Unfortunately, management negotiators are not always well equipped with answers based on principles of labor economics. For example, if new technology (capital) has been used to raise the output level, then the added income that results from the increased productivity may not be immediately available for distribution to labor or stockholders. For the company to experience continued growth in productivity, the cost of new technology must be accounted for and paid prior to raising wages (Rees 1959).

In the long-run analysis, the union negotiator's point of view that increases in productivity are the appropriate criteria against which wage increases should be weighed is correct. However, in the short run, use of increased productivity as a direct measure of the appropriate increase in wages is not correct and will only prove harmful to the company's capability to achieve long-run profitability.

Studies show that union workers do in fact earn higher wages than their nonunion counterparts. H. Gregg Lewis conducted a comprehensive study of union/nonunion wage differences and found a

Table 2.1 1979 Wage Information by Industry Groups

Industry group	Total payroll	Straight-time pay*	Overtime premium pay*	Holiday premium pay	Shift differential
	Average hourly earnings as percent of payroll				
Total, all industries	100.0	93.7	3.6	0.6	0.6
Total, all manufacturing	100.0	92.2	4.2	0.8	0.7
Manufacture of:					
Food, beverages, and tobacco	100.0	92.3	4.8	1.2	0.4
Textile products and apparel	100.0	92.9	4.2	0.7	0.5
Pulp paper, lumber, and furniture	100.0	91.5	4.1	0.3	0.5
Printing and publishing	100.0	94.0	2.6	0.8	0.7
Chemicals and allied products	100.0	91.9	4.8	0.7	0.8
Petroleum industry	100.0	91.3	5.6	1.0	1.1
Rubber, leather, and plastic products	100.0	93.2	3.8	0.6	0.7
Stone, clay, and glass products	100.0	93.7	3.9	0.6	0.4
Primary metal industries	100.0	91.4	4.6	1.3	0.7
Lubricated metal products (excluding machinery and transportation equipment)	100.0	91.8	4.6	1.0	0.5
Machinery (excluding electrical)	100.0	91.1	4.7	0.8	0.8
Electrical machinery, equipment, and supplies	100.0	93.6	3.3	0.6	0.8
Transportation equipment	100.0	90.8	4.9	0.7	1.2
Instruments and miscellaneous manufacturing industries	100.0	94.2	2.9	0.3	0.6
Total, all nonmanufacturing	100.0	95.5	2.8	0.4	0.4
Public utilities (electric, gas, water, telephone, etc.)	100.0	93.8	5.3	0.5	**
Department stores	100.0	97.3	0.8	**	**
Trade (wholesale and other retail)	100.0	94.7	2.7	0.3	0.2
Banks, finance companies, and trust companies	100.0	96.8	1.9	0.2	0.3
Insurance companies	100.0	97.2	1.2	0.1	0.1
Hospitals	100.0	95.4	2.0	0.7	1.4
Miscellaneous nonmanufacturing industries****	100.0	96.2	2.0	0.2	0.1

*Includes bonus or premium pay only. If employee receives $6.00 per hour for straight time and $9.00 for overtime, for each overtime hour worked, $6.00 would be shown as straight-time pay and $3.00 as overtime pay.

**Less than 0.05 percent.

***Less than 0.05¢.

****Includes research engineering, education, government agencies, mining, construction, and so forth.

Source: U.S. Chamber of Commerce, *Employee Benefits, 1979* (Washington, D.C.: Survey Research Center, 1980), p. 25.

Other		Average hourly earnings as cents per hour							Total payroll dollars per year per full-time employee
Earned incentive or production bonus	Other	Total payroll	Straight-time pay	Overtime premium pay*	Holiday premium pay*	Shift differential	Earned incentive or production bonus	Other	
1.1	0.4	731.1	684.7	26.4	4.3	4.0	8.4	3.3	15,191
1.6	0.5	718.0	662.5	30.1	5.5	4.9	11.2	3.8	15,067
1.2	0.1	671.5	620.4	32.0	8.0	2.4	8.1	0.6	14,073
1.3	0.4	515.1	478.4	21.6	3.4	2.7	6.9	2.1	10,610
2.8	0.8	672.6	615.2	27.5	2.3	3.7	18.8	5.1	14,022
1.3	0.6	734.9	690.7	18.8	6.2	4.9	9.8	4.5	14,611
1.3	0.5	789.1	724.4	38.1	5.5	6.2	10.6	4.3	16,383
0.8	0.2	972.4	887.7	54.8	9.7	10.5	7.4	2.3	20,506
1.7	**	637.4	593.9	24.5	4.0	4.2	10.7	0.1	13,174
0.9	0.5	678.3	635.1	26.6	3.9	2.7	6.4	3.6	14,420
1.6	0.4	731.2	668.7	33.9	9.2	4.8	11.9	2.7	15,291
1.8	0.3	682.1	625.6	31.6	6.8	3.6	12.4	2.1	14,626
1.9	0.7	748.0	681.4	35.0	5.6	6.0	14.3	5.7	16,041
1.2	0.5	733.8	686.5	24.0	4.4	5.8	9.1	4.0	15,134
1.4	1.0	809.5	734.5	40.0	6.0	9.8	11.3	7.9	17,090
1.2	0.8	689.0	649.6	19.8	2.0	4.1	8.2	5.3	14,429
0.6	0.3	751.3	717.5	21.2	2.7	2.9	4.5	2.5	15,409
0.1	0.3	877.8	823.8	46.3	4.5	0.1	0.6	2.5	18,389
1.9	**	492.1	478.6	4.1	***	***	9.4	***	9,571
1.5	0.6	641.3	607.2	17.0	2.2	1.0	9.8	4.1	13,392
0.6	0.2	654.8	634.5	12.4	1.3	1.7	3.8	1.1	18,393
0.9	0.5	697.1	678.5	8.4	0.4	0.5	5.9	3.4	13,755
0.1	0.4	576.6	550.5	11.3	4.1	8.0	0.4	2.3	11,911
1.3	0.2	830.8	799.2	16.5	1.6	1.0	10.7	1.8	16,788

Table 2.2 Hourly Compensation 1950 to 1975

Year	Percent relative to 1967
1950	45.0
1951	49.5
1952	52.7
1953	55.7
1954	58.2
1955	60.4
1956	64.3
1957	68.1
1958	71.1
1959	74.0
1960	77.0
1961	79.3
1962	82.5
1963	85.1
1964	88.9
1965	90.9
1966	95.2
1967	100.0
1968	107.0
1969	114.0
1970	121.7
1971	129.8
1972	137.0
1973	147.0
1974	161.7
1975	179.8

Source: Comparative Growth in Manufacturing, Productivity, and Labor Costs in Selected Industrial Countries. Bureau of Labor Statistics Bulletin, 1959 (Washington, D.C.: U.S. Department of Labor, 1977).

relationship between the level of unionism and the wages union workers receive relative to nonunion workers. While the study is somewhat dated for current contract use, the correlation showed unionized workers receive between 10 to 15 percent higher wages (Lewis 1963).

Thomas Kochan (1980) has summarized the more recent results of the numerous other attempts to judge the impact of unions on wage rates:

1. Unions appear to have a more positive effect on the wages of black males than white males. The Ashenfelter study shows that unions increased the wages of black males in 1975 around 22 percent. A study by Duncan of wage growth of young black workers shows that having a union job and staying on that job had a higher return more for black youths than for white youths.

2. The normal age/earning profile of the nonunion sector is leveled by unionization, thus reducing the influence of age and education on earnings. In effect, unions raise the entry-level salaries on union jobs to an amount greater than what an inexperienced younger worker would receive in a comparable nonunion job. At the higher end of the wage spectrum, seniority clauses in union

Table 2.3 Index of Output and Wages per Man-Hour, 1965 to 1978*

	Compensation per man-hour		Output per man-hour	
Year	Private business sector	Nonfarm business sector	Private business sector	Nonfarm business sector
1965	88.6	89.3	95.0	95.9
1970	123.1	121.7	104.2	103.1
1971	131.4	129.9	107.8	106.3
1972	139.7	138.3	111.4	110.1
1973	151.1	149.1	113.6	112.0
1974	164.8	162.7	110.1	108.5
1975	181.2	178.8	112.4	110.5
1976	197.0	193.7	116.4	114.4
1977	213.0	209.3	118.2	115.8
1978	232.7	228.7	118.6	116.4

*1967 = 100.

Source: Productivity Indexes for Selected Industries, 1977 Edition, Bureau of Labor Statistics Bulletin 1983 (Washington, D.C.: U.S. Department of Labor, 1977).

contracts protect more tenured workers from wage erosion after their peak productivity years have passed. By reducing intraoccupational and interoccupational wage dispersion, unions also reduce the effects of education by advocating equal pay for equal work versus equal pay for equally endowed employees.

3. Union wage effects vary across occupations. One study estimated that union laborers earn 42 percent more than their nonunion counterparts. Similarly, union transportation equipment operators earn 38 percent more, with union craftsmen earning 19 percent more and union operatives earning 18 percent more. Union service workers earn 15 percent more than nonunion service workers, and union managers and union clerical employees both earn 2 percent more. Union professionals earn 0.58 percent more than nonunion workers, while union sales workers earn 4 percent less than their nonunion counterparts.

4. The Ashenfelter study showed union wage effects vary across industries. In 1975 estimates for white male blue-collar workers' wages were 43 percent greater than their nonunion counterparts in construction, 16 percent greater for unionized workers in transportation, communications, and utilities, 12 percent greater for unionized workers in nondurable goods manufacturing, and 9 percent in durable goods manufacturing.

5. In firms where blue-collar workers are organized, unions reduce the white-collar/blue-collar wage difference. By promoting wage standardization, they also decrease the effect of intraindustry wage differences. The net effect of unions on wages is to reduce wage inequality among workers. This is because the decrease in wage differences within an industry due to the unions more than offsets any increase in earning differences across industries.

6. Other studies have shown unionization results in larger relative wage effects in less concentrated industries (those with fewer firms in the industry). This fact surfaces because, despite the absence of unionization, concentrated industries pay higher wages than do less concentrated industries.

In addition, unionization leads to increased productivity. A host of studies have shown that unionized companies within the same industry, with other factors held equal, experience 6 to 30 percent greater productivity than their nonunionized counterparts (Oswald 1981). Furthermore, productivity in organized settings tends to be increased by a high enough amount to offset the increase in total costs of higher union wages (Freeman and Medoff 1979). These findings lend strong support to the union negotiators' viewpoint.

DETERMINANTS OF WAGES

Before investigating how to cost wage demands, a review of the basic determinants impacting on wage policy may prove helpful. It is extremely important to develop a strong awareness of the key factors that affect this highly sensitive worker issue—no other area of employment can cause greater emotional response than wage adjustments. While the following delineation of these factors will not qualify the reader to become a labor economist, the review will help alleviate much of the confusion that has kept economists from being able to create effective predictive models in this area.

Area Wage Competition

Competition in the labor market clearly exists, making it necessary for any wage-determination model to allow for variations in local markets. Theory indicates that job worth, as identified through conducting a job analysis and job evaluation, is the criterion for wage determination. Yet market conditions, such as a shortage of workers in a needed skill category, may force a higher wage rate than technical analysis would suggest. Persons costing increases in this area for predictive purposes often use area market wage changes as the standard.

Company Policy

One example of how company policy can affect determination of wages would be following a practice of being a wage leader, that is, paying the highest wages in the local labor market area. This policy is based on the belief that higher productivity can be secured by attracting the best workers in each skill category, which can be accomplished by paying the highest wages. Theoretically, the increased productivity will offset the increased cost of wages. No empirical data currently exist to verify such an assumption.

Another variation of the company policy involves the desire to give employees real wage increases, that is, increases beyond maintenance of purchasing power toward increased living standards. This philosophy is rather common among companies that are attempting to be socially responsible.

It should be kept in mind that the nature of increases tends to be decided through the typical give-and-take bargaining framework. In negotiation situations, the initial costing assumptions rely on economic data regarding cost-of-living changes and estimates from top management as to how much of a real wage increase is desired.

Ability to Pay

An obvious area of importance to the company and to the union is the company's ability to pay. Typically, in times of good sales and profits, little resistance is offered to upward wage and benefit adjustments. When sales and profits drop, management resists these adjustments on the premise that they are unable to pay. Union negotiators offer little argument when sales and profits are good, but can be caught in a serious dilemma when sales and profits are not good. One rationale union negotiators offer for their hesitation to support management's position on the down side is that if concessions in wages are granted to individual companies in a given industry, a competitive advantage is given the inefficient company while the efficient ones are punished. Union negotiators, therefore, tend to maintain a strong position for uniformity.

The "inability to pay" argument is often labeled as bad faith bargaining. The U.S. Supreme Court has ruled that a refusal to substantiate such a claim may be sufficient evidence to support the charge of bad faith (*NLRB* v. *Truitt* 1956). Note that the economic recession of 1981–82 saw an increasing number of companies willing to provide evidence to support the claim of inability to pay.

There are better defenses against providing wage increases than relying on a generalized statement that the company is unable to pay. A more sophisticated, and potentially more effective, defense would include delineation of the specific areas the demand might impact unfairly, including:

1. Its effect on the capital-labor ratio;
2. Changes necessary in product mix;
3. Changes in price-volume relationships;
4. Changes in productivity over the expected life of the demand; and
5. Impact on nonbargaining unit employees.

The important thing to keep in mind is that the effects of a demand go beyond obvious areas. A change in wages, for example, could affect any or all of the above mentioned areas.

Other Determinants

The above determinants have a clearly defined relationship to wage and benefit changes. Other determinants do influence wage negotiations, but their effect is more difficult to measure. Many are in the area of labor economics. Product market influence and industry concentration on wage levels are two examples. Highly concentrated industries (those with a few companies) tend, for instance, to be associated with higher wage levels. There is much disagreement among labor economists regarding these factors and no definitive statements can be made. Therefore, it is acknowledged that other influences may exist; but the emphasis here is on those that can be more clearly defined.

BASIC COSTING TECHNIQUES

There are five commonly accepted basic techniques for costing wage and economic proposals (a combination of techniques may also be used):

1. Total annual cost, which is the total amount spent by a company over a period of time (usually a year) for a given benefit. This figure usually excludes any administrative costs.
2. Cost per employee per year, which is found by dividing the total cost of the benefits by some average number of workers over the time period in question or by the specific number of workers covered by the benefit.
3. Percent of payroll, which is found for the particular benefit in question by dividing the total cost of providing the benefit by the total payroll. The figure to use for total payroll may include all payments to workers or all payments except overtime and shift differentials.
4. Cents per hour is the terminology used to describe the money requested by the union per hour per employee.
5. Cost per hour is found by dividing the total cost of the benefit by total productive hours worked by all employees during the time period.

In preparing for costing wage and economic proposals, it is necessary to gather certain information. A general listing of information that may be required appears in Exhibit 2.1. Note that not all categories will be needed for each of the five techniques.

Total Annual Cost

Knowing the total annual cost of a given benefit is valuable for budgeting, for justifying the existence of the benefit, and for describing the total outlays involved in a benefit program. Thanks to

Exhibit 2.1 General Listing of Information Required to Compute the Cost of Economic Benefits

Number of full-time employees
Number of part-time permanent employees
Number of part-time temporary employees
Number of full-time equivalent employees
Distribution of employees by job title
Distribution of employees by pay grades
Distribution of employees by length of service
Distribution of employees by shift
Number of employees who work seven-day week
Number of employees who work overtime
Number of employees who regularly work Saturday, Sunday, and holidays, who are not seven-day workers
Distribution of employees by number of dependents

computerized accounting systems that can capture these data (which require only minor adjustments), this figure is relatively easy for most companies to obtain. Certain benefits such as pension, profit sharing, and various insurance costs can be easily figured in this manner. Others may not be so easily figured. The true total cost for these other benefits may not be readily available in the more traditional accounting systems. For example, employee discounts on merchandise may show only total discount figures taken, rather than the loss, profit, or added sales necessary to recoup the costs of this benefit.

Cost per Employee per Year

Finding the cost per employee per year for some benefits requires only simple accounting procedures. For example, figures on pay for time not worked, such as vacations and holiday pay, are especially simple to ascertain. Finding individual costs for group health plans and other benefits can be more difficult. These situations require that records of employee participation and the total cost to the company be maintained. From this information, the cost per employee can be obtained by dividing the cost figure by the number of workers participating. For the more easily accrued data where participation of all workers is mandatory, a simple division of cost by total workers will produce the desired figure.

Percent of Payroll

Once all benefit areas are identified and classified, the cost of each benefit category and its own cost as a percentage of total payroll is calculated. Note that careful recordkeeping is necessary for classifying and identifying benefits. In addition, certain key points should be remembered, including:

1. Shift differentials should be excluded from total cost figures unless subject to separate demands.
2. Any planned expansions or contractions of the workforce should be taken into account to adjust the total payroll figure, along with possible change in the "mix of new pay rates."
3. Planned changes in production processes resulting from new technology or equipment that would alter the workforce mix should be taken into account.
4. It is advantageous to determine the cost of a 1 percent wage change. This allows for ease in recomputation during bargaining as demands and counter offers are exchanged and altered.

The percent of payroll technique is the simplest way to figure the cost of a union request, provided it is made in percentage form (such as 5 percent or 10 percent increase for all covered workers). The percentage increase is found by multiplying total dollar payroll of covered workers by the percentage requested. Any planned changes from the current period, such as a change in the number of workers, should be figured into the calculations. Major policy decisions, such as what is to be included as payroll cost, must be made by company management when costing by this technique. Some companies include only straight-time cost, while others include straight time plus any bonus income to be used in computing certain future benefits, such as pensions.

Firms frequently find it advantageous to figure the cost of a 1 percent change in any benefits or wages as a guide for use in contract negotiations. This permits quick and easy computation and recomputation during the negotiation sessions (Heisel and Skinner 1976).

It may be helpful at this point to offer an example for computing a 1 percent cost figure. A sample payroll is displayed in Exhibit 2.2.

Example 2.1: Assume an employer with 300 employees, 200 of whom are covered by the collective bargaining agreement. Using the information provided in Exhibit 2.2, one can determine the cost of a 1 percent wage increase by multiplying the total payroll figure by 1 percent: $3,203,200 X 1 percent = $32,032.

This allows the negotiators to readily determine the impact of any percent increase for all workers. For example, the cost of a demand for a 9 percent increase would be computed by multiplying the 1 percent figure by 9 ($32,032 X 9 = $288,288).

It should be remembered that making this calculation without taking into account the key points listed above may be misleading. By using the existing roster without adjustments, it assumes next year will be a copy of this year's roster, which may not be true.

Consider this example with the addition of certain complications. The $288,288 (9 percent) figure is higher than management would like to spend, yet management recognizes the need for workers to receive an increase of this magnitude. Certain technical changes could make the raise a possibility. This would require, however, that management negotiators work with the appropriate people to ascertain the feasibility of possible improvements. Exhibit 2.3 presents a sample payroll assuming some technical improvements that, while

Exhibit 2.2 Sample Payroll

Job category	Pay rate	Hours work per week	Number weeks worked	Annual wages per worker	Number workers	Total wages
Layout technician	$12.00	40	52	$24,960	10	$ 249,600
Machinist	10.00	40	52	20,800	20	416,000
Assembler	8.00	40	52	16,640	100	1,664,000
Laborer	6.00	40	52	12,480	70	873,600
Total						$3,203,200

Exhibit 2.3 Sample Payroll Costs Incorporating Technical Change

Job category	Salary	Adjusted number workers	Total wages
Layout technician	$24,960	10	$ 249,600
Machinist	20,800	25	520,000
Assembler	16,640	80	1,331,200
Laborer	12,480	60	748,800
Total			$2,847,600

increasing certain skill categories, reduces the overall work force. The resultant reduction is sufficient to enable management to afford the 9 percent demand.

The technical adjustment reduced the number of workers needed from 200 to 175. Moreover, the change resulted in the total wage bill being reduced from $3,203,200 to $2,847,600, a savings of $355,600. Figuring the cost of a 9 percent wage demand shows a savings of $32,004 for the increase:

1 percent cost: $2,847,600 × .01 = $28,476

9 percent increase: $28,476 × 9 = $256,284

w/o technical adjustment	$288,288
w/ technical adjustment	$256,284
Savings	$ 32,004

In this case, the decrease in total wage bill may be sufficient to allow the company to offer the 9 percent increase.

Cents per Hour

Often, union demands for wage increases will be for a certain number of cents per hour to be added to the basic pay rate of each employee. If there are no planned changes in the number of hours to be worked, then simple arithmetic—multiplying the number of hours worked by the cents per hour requested—will give the total increase. However, if changes are planned, then a subdivision of workers by number of hours worked by job category, department, or other management control division will be required.

Exhibit 2.4 Sample Payroll Costs Incorporating 1¢ per Hour Increase

Job category	Hours per week	Number weeks	Number workers	Total hours
Layout technician	40	52	10	20,800
Machinist	40	52	20	41,600
Assembler	40	52	100	208,000
Laborer	40	52	70	145,600
Total				416,000

In addition, the possible impact of the increase on overtime, fringes, and other costs should be checked. Knowing the cost of each 1¢ wage increase will facilitate computing changes in union requests during negotiating sessions.

Exhibit 2.4, which uses the figures from the sample payroll presented in Exhibit 2.2, demonstrates figuring the cost of a 1¢ increase. To arrive at the desired figure, multiply the total number of hours by 1¢ to arrive at the cost for a 1¢ increase. With this figure, the total cost of a given demand can be found by multiplying the number of cents demanded by the figure arrived at above (416,000 × 1¢ = $4,160 for each 1¢ increase granted). If the union requests a 60¢ per hour increase for all covered workers, the total cost of the request would be $4,160 multiplied by 60, or $249,600.

Cost per Hour

Closely aligned to the cents per hour figure, cost per hour information is generally given in cents per hour form. The first requirement in figuring the cost per hour of a benefit is to define the term "hour." It could be defined to mean actual hours worked by employees or by multiplying days of business operation by 8 (8-hour day × 5-day week × 52 weeks = 2,080 hours). There are other configurations of hours that are used. The one used in this book is the scheduled work year, which is the number of weeks worked per year multiplied by the number of hours worked per week. Other methods include:

1. Straight-time productive hours scheduled to the work year minus any paid time off. Paid time includes vacations, holidays, and personal leave time.
2. Total productive time, which is scheduled work plus overtime.
3. Some companies try to hit a medium between scheduled work year and the smaller figure of straight-time productive hours and opt for 2,000 hours.

Note also that many requests for benefits, especially in unionized firms, are presented in a *cents per hour* cost figure (Heisel and Skinner 1976). This form is valuable for informing employees of the cost of benefits because it can easily be related to their hourly pay rate. This technique allows for flexibility and is, therefore, easy to use in bargaining situations. The total cost or impact of the figure can be found by multiplying it times the total hours worked by the employee.

Examples of calculations for cost per hour figures for vacations are provided below. All examples use the formula total cost of vacations divided by the number of hours worked to arrive at the cost per hour figure. Refer to Exhibits 2.4 and 2.5 for data used in examples. For simplicity, it is assumed that all workers are entitled to receive two weeks vacation.

Example 2.2: Cost per hour for vacations using standard method.

$$\frac{\$123{,}200}{416{,}000 \text{ hours}} = 29.6¢ \text{ per hour to the company}$$

Exhibit 2.5 Sample Payroll Costs Incorporating Vacation Benefit

Job category	Hours entitled	Rate pay	Number workers	Total cost
Layout technician	80	$12	10	$ 9,600
Machinist	80	10	20	16,000
Assembler	80	8	100	54,000
Laborer	80	6	70	33,600
Total dollar cost				$123,200

Example 2.3: Cost per hour for vacations using straight-time productive hours cost and assume ten days vacation, seven holidays, and three personal days, or 160 hours.

$$\frac{\$123{,}200}{384{,}000 \text{ hours}} = 32¢ \text{ per hour to the company}$$

(2,080 - 160 = 1,920 X 200 workers = 384,000 hours)

Example 2.4: Cost per hour for vacations using total productive time cost. Assume 100 hours overtime per employee.

$$\frac{\$123{,}200}{436{,}000 \text{ hours}} = 28¢ \text{ per hour to the company}$$

(2,080 + 100 = 2,180 X 200 workers = 436,000 hours)

Example 2.5: Cost per hour for vacations using medium figure, 2,000 hours, worked per employee.

$$\frac{\$123{,}200}{400{,}000 \text{ hours}} = 31¢ \text{ per hour cost to company}$$

The cents per hour cost to the company for this benefit is 29.6¢ or 30¢ per hour. This method of showing benefit costs will be used extensively in later sections when examining total costs of packages employees receive. The alternative cost per hour costing techniques result in costs that range from 30¢ for straight-time productive cost to 28¢ for total productive time cost. The method used may depend on management philosophy or what side of the negotiation table the person is supporting at a given time. As is evident, use of one technique versus another over a range of benefits will result in a somewhat higher or lower cost per hour figure. In this case, a 2¢ difference occurs depending on which method is used, which is a figure difference of $8,320 ($0.02 X 416,000 hours = $8,320). The magnitude of this difference can increase as additional benefits are added to the total compensation package.

Combination of Techniques to Figure a Wage Increase

Consider the familiar possibility of combining a union request for a certain desired percentage increase with a cents per hour minimum.

Exhibit 2.6 Sample Payroll Costs Incorporating Combination of Costing Techniques

Job category	Pay rate	Hours worked per year	Number workers	Total cost	Increase wages	Total cost increase
Layout technician	$12	2,080	10	$ 249,600	10 percent	$ 24,960
Machinist	10	2,080	20	416,000	10 percent	41,600
Assembler	8	2,080	100	1,664,000	80¢	166,400
Laborer	6	2,080	70	873,600	80¢	116,480
Total cost						$349,440

(Note that the limitations described for each particular area still apply.) The general terminology for this type of request is X percent and X number of cents per hour, whichever is greater (for example, 10 percent or 80¢ per hour, whichever is greater). Building on the initial example, if the union should demand 10 percent or 80¢, whichever is greater, wages for all employees in pay categories in excess of $8.00 per hour will be increased on a percentage basis, while wages for those employees in pay categories below $8.00 per hour will be increased on a cents per hour basis (see Exhibit 2.6).

Figuring the demand in this fashion results in an overall increase of 10.9 percent (cost of increase divided by total payroll) or 84¢ per hour (cost of increase divided by total hours worked). An obvious disadvantage to this type of demand is the compression of wage differences between skill levels. Over time, the differences in pay between skill levels tend to narrow substantially, which can lead to worker motivation problems in the higher skill categories.

COST-OF-LIVING ADJUSTMENT CLAUSE

When cost-of-living adjustment (COLA) or escalator clauses first entered into the negotiation forum, they were looked upon by some as enlightened. They provided protection for workers against price increases over and above periodic pay adjustments, which were made according to a formula based on the consumer price index (CPI). This clause increased in popularity with union members to where it is now present in 48 percent of union contracts (BNA 1983). To be more precise, in 1978 contract terms the average unit size covered by a COLA clause was 6,800 workers versus 3,000 without a COLA clause. Escalator provisions are present in 38 percent of agreements in units of 1,000 to 4,999 workers. As it now appears, the larger the bargaining unit, the greater the possibility of COLA coverage. For units of 50,000 to 99,999 workers, COLA coverage is present in 78 percent of the cases, and is present in all contracts with 100,000 workers or more (Sheifer 1979).

At the time COLA clauses first entered the negotiation forum, productivity was growing more rapidly than inflation. Recently, according to many economists, the picture has changed. Price increases and inflation have outdistanced productivity increases, which has resulted in difficult decisions for management negotiators.

The typical adjustment formula calls for some amount per hour adjustment for each measured increase in the CPI. The most frequently used formulas call for 1¢ per hour increases per every 0.3 percent rise in the CPI. This particular ratio is present in 50 percent of contracts

Table 2.4 Table of Wage-Adjusted Provisions for Agreements Covering 1,000 Workers or More (on or after July 1, 1976)

	Agreements	Workers covered
All agreements	1,570	6,741,750
Escalator only	41	275,150
Deferred increase only	592	1,695,100
Reopening only	72	333,350
Escalator and deferred increase	518	2,742,000
Escalator and reopening	4	47,600
Deferred increase and reopening	139	497,500
Escalator, deferred increase, and reopening	131	956,300
No reference to wage adjustments	73	194,750

Source: U.S. Department of Labor Bureau of Labor Statistics–Wage Calendar 1977.

that have a COLA clause. The next most frequent formulas are: 1¢ per every 0.4 percent rise in the CPI (30 percent of contracts); 1¢ per every 0.5 percent increase in the CPI (7 percent of contracts); and 1¢ per every 0.6 percent rise in the CPI (1 percent of contracts) (Bureau of National Affairs [BNA] 1983). The most popular index used is the National All Cities Consumer Price Index.

The COLA or escalator clause is usually combined with some form of deferred wage increase. Bureau of Labor Statistics data shown in Table 2.4 confirm this. Yet, COLAs accounted for 21 percent of all increases going into effect in 1977.

Frequency of adjustment to workers' hourly pay is an important issue to be negotiated. There is a compounding effect of adding the increase, especially when other wage issues such as overtime are considered. Adjustments are most frequently figured on a quarterly basis. Quarterly adjustments are mentioned in 60 percent of contracts with COLA clauses. This is followed by annual adjustments mentioned in 26 percent of contracts (BNA 1983). A small number of agreements are written so that COLAs are paid only when the CPI rises to an agreed-upon figure. Pay adjustments are given for increases above this level.

Cost-of-living adjustments create numerous problems in costing labor contracts. Forces creating the necessity for adjustment tend to be outside the typical areas of management control, for example, changes in the economy. Predicting changes in the economy is an art not yet perfected, as evidenced by the many failures of economists. Labor negotiators can help pinpoint the upper limit of labor cost exposure through establishing upper limits or "caps" for the COLA clauses. The cap on an agreement sets the maximum amount that may be added during each adjustment time period specified in the agreement.

One issue that comes up when dealing with COLAs is whether increases are passed along to consumers. Many private sector companies may pass along all such increases to consumers. However, if a competitor does not have cost-of-living clauses as part of its labor agreement, then to pass on these changes as increases to product price may place a company in a noncompetitive posture. Public sector employers may not have any latitude in passing on such increases. Several cautions need to be highlighted in dealing with caps to these clauses:

1. The cap should be specified for each adjustment period. This avoids exhausting the yearly agreed-upon maximum in any one adjustment period.

2. The impact of the clause on other contract costs should be considered. Careful bargaining regarding whether the clause applies to base pay only or to various fringe benefits, overtime pay, vacation pay, pension, and insurance contributions must be done.

3. If possible companies, especially public sector groups, should avoid signing a contract without a cap.

Example of a COLA Package Figuring

Take an example of a two-year contract period with 10 percent across-the-board wage increase on the original base wage at the start of the first year, and based on the COLA-adjusted figure for the second. The parties can negotiate whether they would prefer to use the adjusted or unadjusted wage rates. The most commonly used COLA formula is 1¢ in base wages for each 0.3 percent quarterly

Exhibit 2.7 COLA Wage Adjustment

Quarterly Adjustment	Change in CPI	Wage increase on COLA	Wage (w/o cap)	Wage (w/cap 4¢)	Wage (w/o COLA)
Beginning wage	–	–	10.00	10.00	10.00
Start, 1st year (10%)	–	–	11.00	11.00	11.00
1st quarter (COLA)	2.1	.07	11.07	11.04	–
2d quarter (COLA)	2.1	.07	11.14	11.08	–
3rd quarter (COLA)	1.5	.05	11.19	11.12	–
4th quarter (COLA)	1.8	.06	11.25	11.16	11.00
Start, 2d year (10%)	–	–	12.38	12.28	12.10
1st quarter (COLA)	2.1	.07	12.45	12.32	–
2d quarter (COLA)	1.2	.04	12.49	12.35	–
3rd quarter (COLA)	1.5	.05	12.54	12.40	–
4th quarter (COLA)	2.4	.08	12.62	12.44	12.10

change in the CPI. Exhibit 2.7 presents COLA wage adjustments using data for the machinist category as presented in Exhibit 2.2. Figures are presented for a 4¢ cap on a quarterly basis, without a 4¢ cap, and for a wage rate without a COLA.

Note from Exhibit 2.7 that the CPI changes totaled 7.5 percent in the first year and 7.2 percent in the second year. Both of these rates are considerably below most recent inflation experience. Yet the wage rate difference is 22¢ per hour between the capped and uncapped COLA wages.

In examining the wage without a COLA column, note that without the inclusion of a COLA clause, the ending wage would have been $12.10. As is currently represented, the COLA added an additional labor cost of 52¢ per hour to the uncapped wages and 34¢ to the capped. This figure might be somewhat higher if wage adjustments were extended to fringe benefits. The magnitude of the differences between the classifications can be large. In this example it could climb to hundreds of thousands of dollars.

Protection Against Inflation

In the ten-year period from 1968 to 1977, the average COLA increase was from 1.6 percent in 1968 and 1969 to 5.8 percent in 1974. During the ten-year period, the COLA adjustments did not match the increase in the CPI in any year (Sheifer 1979). These figures indicate that the COLA clause may not be providing workers with sufficient protection from inflation. Victor Sheifer (1979) offers several reasons why the average COLA clause may not be giving complete compensation protection:

1. Formulas are not sufficient to produce full compensation. The most common formula is a 1¢ increase for each 0.3 point CPI rise.

2. A limit may be placed on the maximum COLA increase. At the beginning of 1978, one-quarter of the workers in major bargaining units with escalation were affected by caps on escalator increases. Annual caps on wage increases over the contract term ranged from less than 1 percent to 6.1 percent, averaging 2.7 percent.

3. Escalator adjustments lag behind price changes. The significance of a lag is related to the pace of inflation. While the lag effect on wage rates may be important in a given year, the long-run impact is on aggregate purchasing power. The degree of lag depends largely on frequency of escalator review.

4. Escalator yields may be diverted. Often, escalator yields are withheld, either permanently or temporarily, to finance supplementary benefits. Approximately 1 million workers are affected in such a manner.

5. Escalators may not operate until a significant CPI rise occurs. For example, contracts covering 100,000 clothing and textile workers yield gains only for CPI rises of more than 7.5 percent in the second contract year and 6 percent in the third.

DIFFERENTIALS, REPORT-IN PAY, AND OVERTIME

Any discussion on wages requires some attention to various forms of supplementary pay. Paying extra for late shifts is required in 83 percent of contracts, and more than likely the absence of a premium in the contract reflects the lack of late shift work (BNA 1983). Shift differential payments generally represent a flat rate in a cents per hour premium for workers who must work other than normal operating times. In a minority of cases, the premium is a percentage of worker pay rates.

Shift differentials tend to be larger for third shifts than for second shifts. The median cents per hour premiums are 25¢ for the third shift and 20¢ for the second shift (up from 15¢ in 1979). In percentage premium terms, these work out to 7 percent for second and 10 percent for the third shift (Bureau of Labor Statistics 1980; BNA 1983).

Employees who report for work but find none available are guaranteed "reporting pay" in 77 percent of contracts. However, in slightly over half of the cases, the guarantee is void if conditions are beyond the control of management. The amount of pay guaranteed varies from one to eight hours overall. Fifty-six percent of contracts guarantee four hours; 13 percent guarantee two hours; and 9 percent guarantee a full eight hours pay (Bureau of Labor Statistics 1980).

Similarly, to cover cases where workers are called in to work at other times than those regularly scheduled, 58 percent of contracts guarantee "call back" or "call in" pay. The amount of pay varies from one hour to eight hours and may have a premium attached to the pay rate (50 percent of contracts provide for a premium to be added to call in pay). The most common guarantee is for four hours found in 70 percent of current contracts (Bureau of Labor Statistics 1980).

Wage increases that are agreed upon will have an added impact if overtime provisions are common. This impact should be figured as part of the cost of any agreed wage increase. Perhaps the most acceptable means found to compute this cost is by using historical data to ascertain what can be expected in the way of overtime hours in the future. Data needed for costing this work should be aggregated by job classification, department, and so forth. The legal standard rate for overtime pay is 1.5 times the normal pay rate. The rate is often up to two times the normal rate in many industries. Proper costing of these data can help companies analyze alternatives, which can include adding part-time employees if these costs are excessive.

MULTIYEAR CONTRACTS

Based on survey results by the Bureau of National Affairs, *Basic Patterns in Union Constraints*, 77 percent of union contracts are for a three-year period. There are advantages to both parties to have the contract period extend for more than one year. For example, longer contract periods allow companies to compute their labor costs for an advance time period. The cost of benefits in a multiyear contract may vary considerably, based on how and when benefit changes are added to workers' pay. That is, a wage increase in effect for only six months will cost half the amount of one in effect for an entire year.

Single-year contracts now make up only 1 percent of the total as compared to 2 percent in 1979 and 5 percent in 1975. Two-year agreements account for 17 percent of labor contracts as compared to 22 percent in 1979. The longer term agreements, those extending four or more years, make up only 4 percent (BNA 1983).

Such things as deferred wage increases are included in 94 percent of contracts, which is up since 1975. Deferred increases include annual improvement factors and productivity increases. Most (8 percent) of the increases take effect the second year of the contract, while only a small group are instituted quarterly or semiannually.

Wage-opener clauses allow for renegotiation of wages during the contract term. These clauses are those not previously discussed that relate to COLA or deferred wage increases. They are found in only 7 percent of contracts (BNA 1983).

Example 2.6: For an example of multiyear contract analysis, assume the union is requesting a two-year contract with a 26 percent increase over

Exhibit 2.8 Total Costs for Sample Wage Increase Patterns Over Multiyear Contracts

Example of spread increase	Beginning total payroll	First year increase (percent)	First year cost	Carryover cost first year	Second year increase (percent)	Second year cost	Total cost example
1	$3,203,200	13	$416,416*	$416,416	13	$470,550*	$1,303,382
2	3,203,200	18	576,576	576,576	8	302,382	1,455,534
3	3,203,200	26	832,832	832,832	0	0	1,665,664

*First year cost computed by following: $3,203,200 × .13 = $416,416.
Second year cost computed: ($3,203,200 + $416,416) × .13 = $470,550.
Total cost of this example: $416,416 + 470,550 + 416,416 = $1,303,382.

the two-year period. There are many ways to divide the increase, but three possibilities prevail:

1. a 13 percent increase in each year of the contract;
2. an 18 percent increase the first year with 8 percent the second; and
3. a 26 percent increase the first year and nothing the second.

Using data from Exhibit 2.2, the costs of the increase in wages can be computed as follows: in the case of the 13 percent increase for each year of the contract, the first year cost equals $3,203,200 × .313 or $416,416; the second year cost equals ($3,203,200 + $416,416) × .13 or $470,550; and the total cost equals $416,416 + 470,550 + 416,416 or $1,303,382.

Exhibit 2.8 presents figures calculated for the 18 percent increase the first year with an 8 percent increase the second, and a 26 percent increase the first year and nothing the second.

A wage increase has an obvious impact on the total cost of any demand. From the above example, the third option with the front-end load is the most expensive. The least expensive is the first option, which spreads the increase in a more even fashion. For union negotiators, the more front-end money they can deliver to the rank-and-file the better. It becomes the management team's job to convince the union that alternative timing of wage increases will still result in satisfying the rank-and-file.

Note that while the union membership would desire a greater amount of money up-front, a two-year contract without a second year increase would not in all probability be desirable. Compensation specialists report that the effect of a raise has limited motivational life, varying from 20 days to perhaps several months. The two-year time span goes well beyond this point.

ADD-ON COST

To complete the costing picture for wages to this point, some discussion about add-on cost becomes essential. What is referred to here as "add-on" cost is also referred to as "roll-up" or "creep" cost. When the 1 percent and 1¢ figures were arrived at earlier, the dollar amount indicated only the cost of straight-time wages. As anyone who has studied the costing problem is aware, the cost of a wage increase involves more than the actual wages themselves. For example, there are certain benefits that increase as wages increase. While the particulars of each benefit-costing technique appear in a later chapter, they are discussed here briefly in conjunction with the concept of add-on cost in figuring an accurate measure of a wage request.

While most companies recognize that an increase in direct wages will result in an increase in other benefit costs, few appear to be systematic in their approach to addressing this issue. That is, many negotiators simply add a fixed percentage to the cost of wages. Survey work by Michael Granof found that companies may not do a complete analysis of these costs and tend to use the same percentage figure year after year. Furthermore, many companies fail to recognize that basing add-on cost increases on historical or last contract figures may be misleading. If fringe benefits are to be negotiated along with direct wage increases, then historical figures may underestimate the true cost of the proposed contract request.

The only value of using current cost data to arrive at a percentage figure to compute add-on cost is to have some price estimate of the total effect of a proposed wage increase. The principal assumption to be understood when using current or historical cost figures is that future benefits will remain the same, percentagewise, as they were in the past.

If the current cost of benefit programs is to serve as an effective guide in developing wage increase agreements, individual add-on figures should be computed for each category as they are agreed upon. Computer facilities in organizations can greatly facilitate this work.

Example 2.7: This example will describe how to calculate add-on costs for the more common programs. Figures from Exhibits 2.2, 2.4, and 2.9 will be used to demonstrate the amount for 1 percent and 1¢ figures that can be used in negotiation.

Exhibit 2.9 indicates that add-on cost will equal almost 30 percent of the straight-time payroll cost. Note that failure to include these figures would result in a 30 percent error in figuring.

The cost of a 1 percent demand is .012998 or .013. This is calculated by adding the percentage of payroll accounted for by benefits to the 1 percent figure. Therefore, the true cost is 1.3¢ for every 1¢ increase. By way of comparison with earlier figures in this chapter:

1. When the 1¢ figure is $32,032 (.01 × 3,203,000), then when add-on costs are taken into account the figure will be $41,641 (.013 × 3,203,000).

Exhibit 2.9 Add-On Cost Figures (dollars)

Benefit	Current cost	Cost per hour
Overtime pay	5,000	.01
Shift differential	14,000	.03
Vacation cost	123,200	.30
Holidays	111,119	.27
Social security	250,000	.60
Unemployment insurance	10,000	.02
Workmen's compensation	25,000	.06
Health insurance*	90,000	.22
Life insurance	21,000	.05
Pensions	300,000	.72
Severance pay	11,000	.03
Total	960,319	2.31

*Changes with wages due to disability rider.
If total straight-time payroll is $3,203,200, then add-on costs are 29.98 percent.

Exhibit 2.10 Effective Pay Rates with Management-Paid Programs (dollars)

Job category	Straight-time pay rate	Straight-time annual	Effective hourly pay ($2.31 added)	Effective annual pay ($4,804 added)
Layout technician	12	24,960	14.31	29,764
Machinist	10	20,800	12.31	25,604
Assembler	8	16,640	10.31	21,444
Laborer	6	12,480	8.31	17,284

2. When the 1¢ figure is $4,160 (.01 X 416,000), then when add-on costs are taken into account the figure will be $5,408 (0.13 X 416,000).

A 9 percent wage demand without add-on adjustment is $288,288. With the adjustment the cost is $374,709, or an $86,481 difference.

The $2.31 per hour figure given is the cost to the company of this benefit package. If 2,080 hours worked per year figure is used, this works out to $4,804.80 (2080 X $2.31) per employee per year in paid benefits. This figure can be of obvious use at the negotiation table. It can then be added to the worker's straight-time pay to display the "effective pay" received. Beyond a useful figure for contract costing and negotiating strategy, compensation specialists suggest it is useful for motivation purposes for employees to know this information.

Not all benefits change with salary or wage levels. Those that do not should be excluded when figuring the true 1 percent or 1¢ figure for negotiation purposes. They should be added back when figuring the final total cost of company benefits and in any transmittals of information showing total effective pay received by employees. For example (see Exhibit 2.10), health insurance was described as changing with pay levels for the example used. However, this figure often does not change with pay levels, but rather is a flat rate per employee. In such cases, it should be excluded when figuring the true figures.

The benefit program used in this example excluded many common benefits companies provide for workers. The impetus to provide these benefits may have come as a result of union initiative, but that is not of concern here. Other items often found include safety equipment, wash-up time, rest periods, lunch periods, jury duty, bereavement, and Christmas gifts. If these are included in the benefit program, their cost should be included when computing the add-on figure.

Some companies separate costs that are required by law and include old-age benefits, survivors' disability, health insurance, unemployment compensation, workmen's compensation, and certain state benefits. The separation exercise should not result in failing to add these figures to the negotiable list to derive the true 1 percent and 1¢ cost figures.

SUMMARY

This chapter is designed to lead the reader through the difficult area of wage costing. It begins by examining the wage-productivity debate, which concerns the fact that wage increases have outpaced productivity gains in recent years. The impact of unions on wage levels is then examined. The first section ends with a look at the basic determinants of wage policy. These include area wage competition, company policy, and ability to pay.

The five basic techniques for costing wages and wage-related items are explained. These include total annual cost, cost per employee per year, percent of payroll, cents per hour, and cost per hour. Examples are given of how to use each technique in costing wages.

Other wage-related items such as cost of living, multiyear contracts, and add-on cost conclude the chapter. Note that while cost-of-living adjustments serve as a way to protect workers from inflation, it is an area where costs can quickly get out of hand when not carefully monitored and may require such elements as an upward adjustment limit. Consider also that multiyear contracts present special problems in negotiations. Changes in pay and benefits can substantially influence the total cost of a collective bargaining agreement.

The final area of discussion concerns add-on costs. These are the summation of benefit items that can equal 30 to 50 percent of straight-time payroll cost. If not included in figuring the total payroll package, large errors can result. The section details how to compute add-on and how to adjust the basic costing techniques to include this significant cost factor.

SKILL-BUILDING EXERCISE

Assume the following information about company X and compute the answers to the questions that follow.

a. Number of employees–500
b. Average rate of pay–$3.00 per hour
c. Overtime rate –$4.50 per hour
d. Paid time off
   1. ten days vacation
   2. six holidays
   3. two days personal leave
e. Overtime–150 hours per employee
f. Scheduled work year–52 weeks X 40 hours per week

1. Figure current straight-time payroll cost.

2. Compute the cost of:

   a. 1 percent wage increase
   b. 1¢ wage increase

3. Total productive hours per employee.

4. Straight-time productive hours.

5. What is the cost per hour to the company of:

   a. ten days vacation for the 500 employees?
   b. six paid holidays?
   c. overtime?

   Compute for the three examples of time worked (scheduled work year hours, straight-time productive, and total productive number of hours).

6. What is the cost of:

   a. 18 percent increase in wages?
   b. 80¢ per hour increase in wages?

7. With the few benefits listed above, what is the true cost of a:

   a. 1 percent increase in wages?
   b. 1¢ increase in wages?

3

Costing Economic Fringe Benefits

INTRODUCTION

Benefit packages in many companies exceed 30 percent of the total payroll cost (Henderson 1979). In a 1979 survey by the U.S. Chamber of Commerce, employee benefits averaged 36.6 percent of payroll costs (1979):

Employer-required payments	9.0 percent
Employer share of pension, insurance, and other agreed-to payments	12.1 percent
Paid rest periods, lunch periods	3.5 percent
Vacations, sick leave, holidays	9.5 percent
Profit-sharing and bonus payments	2.5 percent
Total	36.6 percent

The per-employee benefit figure across all industries equaled $2.68 per hour and $5,560 per year. Table 3.1 displays employee benefits by category and expands on the above five divisions.

Percentages have increased at a dramatic rate over time. For instance, as shown in Table 3.2, the 1929 figure is 3 percent; in 1959 it increased to 19 percent; and in 1969 the package of fringe benefits as a percent of total payroll cost grew to 24 percent. Gross dollar amounts have increased from $1,268 per employee to $6,837 per employee per year from 1959 to 1979 according to longitudinal tracking of 182 companies by the U.S. Chamber of Commerce. Data are presented in Table 3.3. This amounts to a 439 percent increase.

Table 3.1 Employee Benefits by Category

Type of benefit	Total all companies	Total all manufacturing	Total nonmanufacturing
Total employee benefits as percent of payroll	36.6	37.2	35.7
1. Legally required payments (employer's share only)	9.0	10.1	7.6
a. Old-age, survivors', disability, and health insurance (FICA taxes)	5.8	5.9	5.6
b. Unemployment compensation	1.5	1.9	1.0
c. Workers' compensation (including estimated cost of self-insured)	1.7	2.3	0.9
d. Railroad retirement tax, railroad unemployment and cash sickness insurance, state sickness benefits insurance, etc.**	*	*	0.1
2. Pension, insurance, and other agreed-upon payments (employer's share only)	12.1	12.1	12.1
a. Pension plan premiums and pension payments not covered by insurance-type plan (net)	5.4	4.7	6.4
b. Life insurance premiums; death benefits; hospital, surgical, medical, and major medical insurance premiums, etc. (net)	5.7	6.6	4.4
c. Salary continuation or long-term disability	0.3	0.3	0.3
d. Dental insurance premiums	0.3	0.3	0.2
e. Discounts on goods and services purchased from company by employees	0.1	*	0.2
f. Employee meals furnished by company	0.1	*	0.3
g. Miscellaneous payments (compensation payments in excess of legal requirements, separation or termination pay allowances, moving expenses, etc.)	0.2	0.2	0.3

3. Paid rest periods, lunch periods, wash-up time, travel time, clothes-change time, get-ready time, etc.	3.5	3.6	3.4
4. Payments for time not worked	9.5	8.8	10.2
a. Paid vacations and payments in lieu of vacation	4.7	4.5	4.8
b. Payments for holidays not worked	3.2	3.2	3.1
c. Paid sick leave	1.2	0.8	1.8
d. Payments for state or national guard duty; jury, witness, and voting pay allowances; payments for time lost due to death in family or other personal reasons, etc.	0.4	0.3	0.5
5. Other items	2.5	2.6	2.4
a. Profit-sharing payments	1.4	1.6	1.2
b. Contributions to employee thrift plans	0.3	0.2	0.4
c. Christmas or other special bonuses, service awards, suggestion awards, etc.	0.4	0.5	0.3
d. Employee education expenditure (tuition refunds, etc.)	0.2	0.1	0.3
e. Special wage payments ordered by courts, payments to union stewards, etc.	0.2	0.2	0.2
Total employee benefits as cents per payroll hour	267.6	267.1	268.2
Total employee benefits as dollars per year per employee	5,560	5,605	5,501

*Less than 0.05 percent.
**Figure shown is considerably less than legal rate because most reporting companies had only a small proportion of employees covered by tax.
Source: Employee Benefits, 1979 (Washington, D.C.: Chamber of Commerce of the United States, Survey Research Center, 1980), p. 8.

Table 3.2 Growth of Benefits, 1929 to 1979
(percent of wages and salaries)

Type of payment	1929	1959	1956	1979
1. Legally required	0.8	4.2	6.6	9.4
Old-age, survivors', disability, and health insurance (FICA taxes)	0	1.7	3.5	4.8
Unemployment compensation	0	0.9	0.7	1.2
Workers' compensation	0.6	0.6	1.0	1.0
Government employee retirement	0.2	0.8	1.1	2.1
Other	0	0.2	0.3	0.3
2. Agreed-upon	0.4	4.2	5.1	8.1
Pensions	0.2	2.6	2.7	3.6
Insurance	0.1	1.3	2.1	4.1
Other	0.1	0.3	0.3	0.4
3. Rest periods	1.0	3.0	3.3	3.8
4. Time not worked	0.7	6.6	7.7	9.6
Vacation	0.3	3.5	3.9	4.8
Holidays	0.3	2.2	2.7	3.2
Sick leave	0.1	0.8	0.9	1.2
Other	0	0.1	0.2	0
5. Bonuses, profit-sharing, etc.	0.1	1.0	1.3	1.1
Total benefit payments	3.0	19.0	24.0	31.8

Note: Data in this table are not comparable with Tables 3.1 or 3.3 because of different sample sizes.

Source: Employee Benefits, 1979 (Washington, D.C.: Chamber of Commerce of the United States, Survey Research Center, 1980), p. 30.

The increase in total benefits can be tied in part to the higher cost of individual benefits. In addition, new benefits have been added, including those required by federal, state, and local statutes. Another factor impacting on the increase in benefits is the role benefit packages can have in improving employee perceptions of well-being and, therefore, in improving productivity for the company.

Research in the field suggests, however, that companies may not be getting the return they expect on this form of investment. One reason may be that employees often place minimal value on these benefits, take them for granted, or do not consider them as incentives for increased productivity (Henderson 1979). This may be due to a failure to communicate the value of benefits to employees in a detailed and clear manner. This, in turn, may be due to the fact that many companies have not performed a sufficient cost analysis of the benefit packages and, therefore, do not have accurate figures to convey to employees (Henderson 1979). Knowing the cost of a benefit package is essential before communication with employees can take place, not to mention its importance in determining the long-range impact of benefit costs on company operations and making appropriate management decisions in labor contract negotiations.

Union negotiators must also assume responsibility for costing demands in this area. Full analysis by the union team guards against irresponsible demands and arms it with reliable data to use in arguing a given position.

Fringe benefits and certain noneconomic benefits may constitute nonproductive time payments. There is no doubt that vacations, holidays, and other benefits are reasonable, or that a longer break may increase employee productivity. The focus of attention in this chapter is to learn how to cost these benefits, a subject that has not received sufficient attention in the field of labor relations.

Ideally, testing would be undertaken to find the impact of benefits on productivity levels. In a real-world situation, this would not be possible. However, demands for benefits are a fact of life and the assumption is that they have a positive effect on productivity. Therefore, both company and union negotiators must arm themselves with the necessary skills to cost these programs.

The following sections address various techniques for costing benefits. An attempt is made to include many of the familiar benefits. Similar types of benefits not mentioned specifically may have a costing format in common with those mentioned. Understanding the basic format will enable the negotiator to cost benefits not addressed specifically by using the technique for a similar type of benefit.

COSTING HOLIDAY PAY

It is common for companies to offer employees from nine to 12 paid holidays per year. The median number is ten, which is up from

Table 3.3 Comparison of Benefits of 182 Companies from 1959 to 1979

Item	1959	1961	1963	1965	1967	1969	1971	1973	1975	1977	1979
All industries (182 companies)											
1. As percent of payroll, total	24.4	25.8	26.8	27.1	29.1	31.0	33.0	35.1	37.6	39.9	41.2
a. Legally required payments (employer's share only)	3.5	4.0	4.4	4.2	4.9	5.3	5.6	6.6	7.0	7.6	8.2
b. Pension, insurance, and other agreed-upon payments (employer's share only)	8.4	8.6	9.0	9.3	9.8	10.4	11.6	12.2	13.4	14.6	15.1
c. Paid rest periods, lunch periods, etc.	2.1	2.4	2.4	2.5	2.8	3.1	3.2	3.3	3.7	3.7	3.7
d. Payments for time not worked	8.3	8.7	9.0	9.1	9.5	10.1	10.5	10.7	11.2	11.5	11.7
e. Profit-sharing payments, bonuses, etc.	2.1	2.1	2.0	2.0	2.1	2.1	2.1	2.3	2.3	2.5	2.5
2. As cents per payroll hour	61.3	69.6	78.5	85.1	99.9	117.0	140.7	173.0	219.1	261.3	328.2
3. As dollars per year per employee	1,268	1,443	1,626	1,770	2,071	2,441	2,919	3,628	4,563	5,416	6,837
All manufacturing (73 companies)											
1. As percent of payroll, total	23.2	24.8	25.7	26.5	29.0	31.2	33.6	35.9	39.0	41.0	42.5
a. Legally required payments (employer's share only)	3.9	4.5	4.9	4.6	5.4	5.9	6.4	7.5	8.0	8.6	9.2
b. Pension, insurance, and other agreed-upon payments (employer's share only)	7.2	7.4	7.7	8.2	9.1	10.0	11.5	12.4	13.7	14.7	15.3

c. Paid rest periods, lunch periods, etc.	2.6	3.1	3.1	3.3	3.5	3.7	3.9	3.9	4.1	4.2	4.2
d. Payments for time not worked	7.0	7.5	7.8	8.3	8.7	9.3	9.8	10.0	10.6	11.0	11.3
e. Profit-sharing payments, bonuses, etc.	2.5	2.3	2.2	2.1	2.3	2.0	2.0	2.1	2.6	2.5	2.5
2. As cents per payroll hour	59.2	67.6	75.5	83.2	98.1	116.7	142.8	174.4	221.9	264.1	339.2
3. As dollars per year per employee	1,228	1,410	1,585	1,768	2,068	2,482	3,017	3,724	4,689	5,505	7,157
All nonmanufacturing (109 companies)											
1. As percent of payroll, total	25.2	26.5	27.5	27.4	29.1	30.9	32.6	34.5	36.7	39.2	40.3
a. Legally required payments (employer's share only)	3.2	3.6	4.1	3.8	4.6	4.9	5.1	6.0	6.3	6.9	7.5
b. Pension, insurance, and other agreed-upon payments (employer's share only)	9.2	9.5	9.9	10.0	10.2	10.8	11.6	12.1	13.1	14.5	14.8
c. Paid rest periods, lunch periods, etc.	1.8	2.0	1.9	1.9	2.4	2.6	2.8	2.9	3.5	3.5	3.5
d. Payments for time not worked	9.2	9.5	9.7	9.7	10.0	10.6	10.9	11.1	11.6	11.9	12.0
e. Profit-sharing payments, bonuses, etc.	1.8	1.9	1.9	2.0	1.9	2.0	2.2	2.4	2.2	2.4	2.5
2. As cents per payroll hour	62.7	70.9	80.6	86.4	101.1	117.2	139.3	172.1	217.3	259.4	320.9
3. As dollars per year per employee	1,294	1,464	1,654	1,771	2,073	2,413	2,854	3,564	4,478	5,357	6,623

Note: Data in this table are not comparable with Tables 3.1 or 3.2 due to different sample sizes.
Source: Employee Benefits, 1979 (Washington, D.C.: Chamber of Commerce of the United States, Survey Research Center, 1980), p. 27.

nine in prior years (Bureau of Labor Statistics 1980). Prior to the recession in 1982, there was a trend toward increasing the number of paid holidays. Various labor agreements signed during the recession, which was a period of reverse collective bargaining, actually reduced the number of holidays. It is difficult to judge if the future trend will be toward increasing or decreasing the number of employee holidays. In addition, some companies offer from one to three floating holidays, to be chosen by the employee or by mutual agreement with the employer.

Most Commonly Offered Holidays

New Year's
Good Friday
Memorial Day
Independence Day
Labor Day
Thanksgiving Day
Christmas Day

Other Common Days

Washington's Birthday
Columbus Day
Presidential Election Day
Veterans' Day
Friday after Thanksgiving
Christmas Eve
New Year's Eve

Employees often can work on the holiday for extra pay. It is generally recommended that employee eligibility for holiday or premium pay for working a holiday be contingent upon the employee working the days before and after. The rationale when the employee is taking the holiday is to reduce the possibility of a holiday's extending into a minivacation, which can create numerous staffing problems. The rationale when the employee is working the holiday is to preclude the employee's taking a day off, working the holiday, and earning two days' pay.

In addition, when the regulars are not working, it may be necessary to recruit replacement workers. The cost of these workers must be included in the cost of the benefit. Again, accurate records regarding the historical impact of holidays and any overtime or replacement help needed can be used as predictors of future cost.

According to Michael Granof (1973), there are other expenses involved with holiday pay (as there are with sick pay and paid vacations) that are frequently overlooked. For the most part, computing the cost of hiring temporary help includes only the wage paid multiplied by the number of hours worked. Yet there are other costs that are often overlooked, including:

- advertising
- references
- employment agencies
- letter of application
- application blanks
- interview by personnel
- security and credit investigation
- company badges and safety equipment
- indoctrination and training
- break-in time
- severance pay
- extra Social Security taxes
- insurance cost
- increased unemployment

Computing the Cost of the Holiday Benefit

Building on the cost-per-hour model used in the previous chapter, the cost of a holiday benefit for a company that allows ten days of paid holiday time annually will be computed. Using the data in Exhibit 3.1, the cost of current worker holiday benefits at straight-time pay rates can be calculated. No allowance was made in Exhibit 3.1 for other possible cost items such as advertising, personnel department indoctrination and training, and so forth. In actual work situations, where more complete information is available, estimates in these areas could be made. Without these added items, the straight cost per hour of this benefit is almost 30¢.

Exhibit 3.1 Costing Holiday Pay

Job category	Number of workers	Rate of pay	Number of holidays	Hours per day	Cost
Layout technician	10	$12	10	8	$ 9,600
Machinist	20	10	10	8	16,000
Assembler	100	8	10	8	64,000
Laborer	70	6	10	8	33,600
Total cost					$123,200

Example 3.1: 200 workers × 2,080 hours = 416,000 hours

$$\text{Cost/hour benefit} = \frac{\text{Total cost}}{\text{Number hours worked}}$$

$$= \frac{\$123{,}200}{416{,}000} = 29.6¢$$

One can take this example and arrive at another way to look at the cost of this benefit. How much will sales have to increase to cover the cost of the holiday benefit? If the gross margin of this company is assumed to be 25 percent, then $492,800 in additional sales would be needed to offset this cost. To compute this figure, the total cost of the benefit is divided by the gross margin figure.

$$\text{Sales required to offset benefit cost} = \frac{\text{Total cost benefit}}{\text{Gross margin}}$$

$$= \frac{\$123{,}200}{.25}$$

$$= \$492{,}800$$

Any additions to the holiday benefit would increase the required sales figure. Company negotiators need to reciew long-range sales forecast and economic data to be sure whatever figure agreed upon is in line with sales projections. In later sections, break-even analysis is discussed as it relates to this and other issues. The added sales figures (units produced to reach this dollar amount) based on current operating methods may not be as profitable. Depending on the industry, use of figures other than gross margin may be more appropriate. For example, in the grocery business, sales turnover figures may present a more accurate result than gross margin. In addition, the gross margin figure may overstate or understate the issue, depending on whether the viewpoint is that of the labor or the management negotiator. It is, however, a useful figure for rule-of-thumb illustrative purposes.

Costing an Additional Holiday

If one assumes the union request is for an additional holiday for all covered workers in the coming contract, the lost production can be assumed to be made up by overtime. To figure the cost accurately, the union request of a 10 percent wage increase will also be figured into the computation.

Example 3.2:

	Total cost	Cents/hour
Current cost of ten days of paid holiday benefit	$123,200	29.6
10 percent wage increase	12,320	.03
Cost of current benefit w/o added day	$135,520	

Additional holiday cost (assume 1.5 times normal pay rate for overtime, plus 10 percent wage increase)

*Layout technician: 10 workers X $19.80 X 8 hours	=	$1,584.00
Machinist: 20 workers X $16.50 X 8 hours	=	2,640.00
Assembler: 100 workers X $13.20 X 8 hours	=	10,560.00
Laborer: 70 workers X $9.90 X 8 hours	=	5,544.00
Total cost of one new holiday	=	$20,328.00

*12.00 X 110 = 13.20 at 1.5 rate base for overtime = 19.80

$$\text{Cost/hour of added day} = \frac{\$20{,}328}{416{,}000 \text{ hours}} = 48.0$$

New total cost of holiday benefit

Current ten days w/10 percent increase	$135,520
Additional holiday	20,328
New total cost of 11-day holiday benefit	$155,848
Cents/hour cost	37.0

The request of an additional holiday at the proposed wage rate results in a 21 percent increase in the cost of this benefit from current levels. In total dollars, this comes to a $20,328 increase or an additional 5¢ per hour.

COSTING PAID VACATIONS

A key benefit in the area of pay for nonproductive time is the granting of annual vacations to employees. Any method of computing the cost for this benefit depends on the manner of compensating the employee. Those who receive a regular salary will receive this as their vacation benefit (Henderson 1979). However, those who are paid on an incentive basis may receive only what would be their "draw" amount, or have their pay based on some average earnings for some time frame before the vacation.

Eligibility for vacation is normally based on tenure periods of employees: one week vacation after six months of service, two weeks for one to three years of service, and so forth. Table 3.4 illustrates overall industry tenure requirements for vacation benefits. To calcu-

Table 3.4 Length of Service Requirements for Vacation Allowance

	Length of vacation allowance–Number of agreements					
Length of service	1 week	2 weeks	3 weeks	4 weeks	5 weeks	6 weeks
6 months	157	7	–	–	–	–
1 year	709	307	17	–	–	–
2 years	1	377	15	–	–	–
3 years	1	315	28	3	–	–
5 years	–	49	212	16	–	–
10 years	–	2	748	101	10	1
12 years	–	–	16	59	3	–
15 years	–	1	29	473	28	3
20 years	–	–	–	329	293	9
25 years	–	–	–	14	380	66
30 years	–	–	–	1	35	119

Note: Total number agreements: 1,550. Total with vacation: 1,401. Table indicates time when employee first becomes eligible for vacation benefit. Figures may represent range of eligibility.

Source: Bureau of Labor Statistics, Bulletin 2095, May 1981, U.S. Department of Labor, Washington, D.C., p. 83.

late the cost of this benefit, it becomes necessary to keep accurate records of the employee work force in terms of length of service on the job and pay schedule. In addition, it is necessary to have knowledge regarding how vacation periods are determined and the length of benefit for each employee.

To determine the true cost of this benefit, it is necessary to know whether vacationing employees will be replaced with temporary employees. This implies calculating the cost per hour of the replacement, which involves the base rate of pay; the prorated cost of recruiting, testing, and so forth; plus any fringe benefits for temporary workers, such as Social Security, workmen's compensation, and a group of benefits not required by law but agreed to by management. To determine the long-run cost implications of these benefits, certain questions must be answered: Can an employee accumulate benefits over a period of years and receive the benefit upon retirement? Can the employee receive extra pay by working instead of taking the vacation? Do part-time and nonexempt workers qualify for vacation benefits? In retailing, for example, most firms do grant vacations to all employees (Gable and Hollon 1977).

Vacation clauses for workers appear in 91 percent of all contracts. Most recent BNA surveys reveal the trend toward five- and six-week vacations and reduced requirements for service time to the company to qualify. One-week vacations are less frequent than two-, three-, or four-week vacations, due to more contracts providing for a minimum of two weeks for all employees, regardless of tenure. Eighty-three percent of contracts state the basis for computing vacation pay. Slightly more than half of contracts pay at base rate of pay and one-third pay on employee average earnings (BNA 1983; Major Collective Agreements 1980).

Computing the Cost of Vacation Pay

Building on the model used above, cost per hour of the vacation benefit will be calculated. The minimum vacation time will be two weeks and the maximum four weeks. Assumed vacation times can be found in Exhibit 3.2.

Example 3.3:

$$\text{Cost per hour of the holiday benefit} = \frac{\text{Total cost}}{\text{Number hours}} = \frac{\$185{,}440}{416{,}000} = 44.6¢$$

In the example, almost 45¢ per hour is spent by the company on vacation costs. This figure is understated to the extent that the only cost included is straight-time pay. If the company or union negotiators were to address the problem of sales required to cover this benefit (assuming again a 25 percent gross margin), the figure would be $741,760.

The 45¢ figure, when added to the straight-time rate, communicates a total compensation figure to employees (that is, the total package of wages and benefits gathered to represent the true effective wage level). However, there is another level at which these costs must be viewed and reported. In some instances, not every vacationing employee needs to be replaced for short periods. Other workers may be needed to perform essential job duties that cannot be done within the normal time. In these cases, the true cost of a vacation

Exhibit 3.2 Total Cost of the Vacation Benefit

Job category	Number of workers	Pay rate	Vacation entitlement: 2 weeks (80 hrs)	3 weeks (120 hrs)	4 weeks (160 hrs)	Number of hours entitled	Total cost
Layout technician	10	$12	3	4	3	1,200	$ 14,400
Machinist	20	10	6	8	6	2,464	24,640
Assembler	100	8	30	40	30	12,000	96,000
Laborer	70	6	25	20	25	8,400	150,400
Total cost*							$185,440

*No adjustments have been made for other cost factors in temporary replacements recruiting, testing, and benefits due.

Exhibit 3.3 Replacement Vacation Cost

Job category	Number of workers	Number replaced	Replacement cost rate	Number of hours replaced**	Cost of replacement
Layout technician	10	10	$13.44*	1,200	$ 16,128
Machinist	20	15	11.20	1,800	20,160
Assembler	100	65	8.96	8,000	71,680
Laborer	70	30	6.72	3,600	24,192
Total cost					$132,160

*$1,200 × 1.12 = $13.44 with 12 percent premium.
**Figures for hours for these workers are assumed over an even distribution of categories with excess going to those with longer tenure.

benefit is the replacement figure plus the original worker's salary for that time.

If the company can schedule vacations so that only 60 percent of vacationing workers need be replaced, rather than 100 percent as is implied above, the cost configuration would be different. To illustrate, assume that the 120 replaced workers are distributed among the four job categories (see Exhibit 3.3). Assume a 12 percent pay premium to cover the cost of temporary or replacement workers, recruitment, personnel costs, and statutory fringe benefits. The $132,160 replacement cost figure is for current wage rates. If wages are expected to increase, then the increase level should be figured into the cost. If the union is demanding a 10 percent increase, the adjusted figures would be the following:

Example 3.4:

Current total cost for all workers	$185,440	cents/hour	45¢
with 10 percent increase	$203,984	cents/hour	49¢
Replacement vacation cost	$132,160	cents/hour	32¢
with 10 percent increase	$145,376	cents/hour	35¢

Exhibit 3.4 Adjusted Vacation Schedule Reflecting Added Vacation Time Based on Existing Eligibility

Job category	Number of workers	Current vacation plan			Proposed vacation plan		
		2 weeks	3 weeks	4 weeks	2 weeks	3 weeks	4 weeks
Layout technician	10	3	4	3	1	5	4
Machinist	20	6	8	6	30	10	7
Assembler	100	30	40	30	15	45	40
Laborer	70	25	20	25	10	30	30

Compression of Vacation Eligibility

Compression, which refers to the process of reducing tenure requirement for eligibility for benefits, is an increasingly important point for negotiators. Consider a union request for a change in the benefit plan making workers eligible for additional weeks of paid vacation. Exhibit 3.4 assumes some form of compression demand and also includes an allowance for the increase in wages demanded.

Exhibit 3.5 Total Cost of Compression Demand

Job category	Pay rate w/10 percent increase	Number vacation hours entitled**	Total cost
Layout technician	$13.20*	1,320	$ 17,424
Machinist	11.00	2,560	28,160
Assembler	8.80	13,000	114,400
Laborer	6.60	9,200	60,720
Total			$220,704

*$12.00 × 1.10 percent = $13.20.

**Distribution weeks in Exhibit 3.3: 2 weeks = 80 hours, 3 weeks = 120 hours, 4 weeks = 160 hours.

The example will cost on a total replacement basis and a replacement cost basis with a 12 percent premium.

In total cost figures, the compression demand with a 10 percent increase amounts to a $33,152 or an 18 percent increase in cost to the company (see Exhibit 3.5). This compression demand resulted in 35 added weeks of paid vacation eligibility. This is without increasing the total possible vacation time beyond four weeks.

Example 3.5:

$$\text{Cost per hour of compression demand} = \frac{\text{Total cost benefit}}{\text{Number hours worked}} = \frac{220{,}704}{416{,}000} = 53 \text{ cents/hour}$$

Added Weeks of Vacation Benefit

It is not uncommon during normal economic conditions for additional vacation weeks to be requested in negotiation situations. There

Exhibit 3.6 Replacement Vacation Cost—Two Added Weeks of Vacation (based on compression demand, 10 percent increase wages, 12 percent premium)

Job category	Number of workers replaced	Replacement cost rate	Current entitlement*	Union*** proposed entitlement (weeks) 2	3	4	5	6	Number of hours replaced	Cost
Layout technician	10	$14.64**	1,200	1	3	2	2	2	1,640	$ 24,009
Machinist	15	12.20	1,800	2	5	4	3	1	2,240	27,328
Assembler	65	9.76	8,000	10	25	20	7	3	9,120	89,011
Laborer	30	7.32	3,600	5	10	8	4	3	4,400	32,208
Total										$172,556

*See Exhibit 3.2.
**$12.00 + 10 percent wage increase + 12 percent premium = $14.64.
***Hypothetical figuring of entitlement for the change in vacation time.

are obvious problems in scheduling the added weeks. The cost of vacations is figured on a 60 percent replacement basis, using a 12 percent premium cost for the temporary or replacement workers, and a 10 percent increase in wages. The union request is for two added weeks of vacation time, which will be a fifth or sixth week of paid vacation. The distribution is arbitrary.

Exhibit 3.6 takes on some significance when compared to Example 3.4. The cost in Example 3.4 was 32¢ per hour without a 10 percent increase, and 35¢ with the 10 percent increase. Extending the vacation schedule to include two additional weeks results in the cost per hour rising to 41¢ or a $40,396 increase to satisfy the union request.

COSTING PENSIONS AND PROFIT SHARING

Pensions and profit sharing are areas for which the advice and counsel of specialists are not just helpful, but mandatory. Early pension and profit-sharing payments were not nearly so complicated as they are now. Currently, they must provide decent retirement benefits and simultaneously satisfy numerous requirements of both federal and state agencies and laws. Pension plans are incorporated into 90 percent of contracts and, along with Social Security cost, account for some 35 percent of the total cost of all benefits offered by a company (Henderson 1979 and Granof 1973).

For pension cost to be a legitimate deductible business expense on employer taxes, they must qualify according to various Internal Revenue Codes. In addition, the Employee Retirement Income Security Act of 1974 (ERISA) mandates that many tough provisions be included in pension plans. If the company is unionized, then the employer must also permit its union to have a voice in the plan's administration.

Currently, according to Belcher (1974), most plans fall into a few forms. These are group pensions, deferred or cash profit sharing, and savings plans.

1. Group pensions are the basic model, and are frequently combined with profit-sharing and savings plans. Normally included is mandatory coverage of all employees and is either paid in total by company or some form of cost sharing with the employees.

2. Profit-sharing plans, deferred or cash, normally involve setting aside certain amounts of company profit for each employee. Upon the retirement, death, or other agreed-upon circumstances, the benefits are distributed to the employees or their chosen beneficiaries. Tax advantages and accrued interest make these plans attractive to employees. The ultimate test of their usefulness as an incentive depends in large measure on the vesting provisions. Vesting time is the amount of time an employee must be working before having full rights to the funds. A very famous example of deferred distribution is the Sears & Roebuck plan that has worked very well to provide satisfactory retirement benefits and has also worked effectively as an employee incentive.

Cash or current profit-sharing plans (not as popular as deferred plans) represent about 40 percent of total profit-sharing arrangements. Normally found in smaller organizations, the funds are paid out as soon as possible after profits are earned. Usually the distribution is made monthly or quarterly. It has been estimated that 75,000 cash plans were in effect in 1971 versus over 100,000 deferred plans.

3. Savings plans are used to stimulate employee savings for retirement. The incentive provided by the company is in some form of matching funds, which range from 50 to 100 percent of employee contributions to the plan. These plans have a stated limit, which is usually in a range of 5 to 10 percent of the employee base pay. The funds are then placed in one of various types of investment arrangements.

Generally, the cost of any proposed changes in pension plans are given to consulting or staff actuaries. Companies provide the necessary demographic data and the cost of the plan is based on the traditional techniques used by actuary companies and quoted in terms of total annual cost or a cents per hour figure. What the company outlay will be depends on the actuarial cost-method used. The "entry-age normal method," which assumes a standard entry age, is the most widely used technique. Benefits are usually amortized over 30 years (Granof 1973).

Companies must always be careful in adjusting benefits without a thorough examination of all ramifications. Two examples offered by Heisel and Skinner (1976) reinforce this fact. First, if a company decides to help persons already retired by changing the plan to allow for postretirement adjustment to reflect Consumer Price Index (CPI) increases, it may be difficult to project accurate costs. This sort of change makes it hard for consulting actuaries to give the company accurate figures as to what pension costs will be in the future. Second, any automatic wage adjustment added to help current employees keep pace with changes in economic conditions will make it very difficult to predict wage levels at retirement. The wage-level prediction at retirement is the key point of information in determining both future benefits and company contribution level to provide such benefits.

In addition to the above, Heisel and Skinner (1976) suggest various other questions that should be considered when costing pension benefits:

1. Will the employee share in pension cost? Will his contribution be funded immediately and be "portable" to go with the employee when leaving the company?
2. What is the relationship of benefits to length of service? Are there any provisions for early retirement?
3. When will the employee have full right to the contribution of the employer? (Certain legislation requires private plans to provide vesting according to various formulas.)

Actuaries tend not to offer opinions on the efficacy of company policy. Their input is of a technical nature: they figure the cost of company plans and plan changes. The company must decide, for example, whether it will provide continuing benefits during periods when senior employees are laid off. Company policy also tends to dictate the minimum plan benefits, that is, how retirement benefits will be paid.

Age 65 is specified as normal retirement age in 91 percent of the plans. The range varies from 55 to 70 years. Minimum service require-

Exhibit 3.7 Computing Pension Cost

Job category	Number of employees	Wage rate	Total wages	Total cost
Layout technician	10	$12	$ 249,600 × .1	$ 24,960
Machinist	20	10	416,000 × .1	41,600
Assembler	100	8	1,664,000 × .1	166,400
Laborer	70	6	873,600 × .1	87,360
Total				$320,320

ment is specified in 58 percent of contracts. These range from five to 25 years, with 66 percent requiring ten years of service, and only 7 percent requiring 25 years of service (BNA 1983).

Exhibit 3.7 shows calculations for costing pension benefits. The employer contribution is assumed to be 10 percent of an employee's base wage rate. The cost per hour of this benefit is 77¢ to the company. To have some idea as to what would be necessary in terms of sales dollars necessary to cover this cost, the same formula applies as before. At a 25 percent gross margin, the requirement is $1,281,280 for this benefit.

Example 3.6:

$$\text{Cost per hour pension benefit} = \frac{\text{Total cost benefit}}{\text{Number hours}}$$

$$= \frac{\$320,320}{416,000 \text{ hours}}$$

$$= 77¢$$

What if the union demands a plan improvement of an added 1 percent increase in employer contribution? To compute this demand, information is also needed regarding any proposed wage increase. For simplicity, the wage change is given as an across-the-board increase of 10 percent.

Example 3.7:

1. Current payroll = $3,203,200
2. Wage increase 10 percent = 320,320
3. New payroll cost (a + b = c) = $3,523,520

4. Pension 11 percent (c × 11 percent = d) = 387,587

$$\text{Cost per hour of new pension} \quad \frac{\$387,587}{416,000 \text{ hours}}$$

= 93¢

5. Increase in cost of 1 percent demanded range = $67,267

This results in a 21 percent increase in benefit cost to the company for the union request. To recapture the 1 percent increase, an additional \$269,068 is required, bringing the total to \$1,550,348. In the basic language of cents per hour, the change is 16¢ added to the cost per hour of this benefit, raising the hourly cost figure to 93¢.

COSTING LIFE INSURANCE

Life insurance protection for employees is provided by almost every company. The BNA study showed that life insurance is present in 98 percent of manufacturing and 93 percent of nonmanufacturing contracts analyzed. The cost of the coverage is paid by the company in most cases. The BNA study showed that 87 percent of benefit plans were paid for by the company, while the cost is shared in 13 percent of the cases (BNA 1983).

Many types and varieties of insurance plans are available, including group life, health and hospitalization, dental and vision, disability, legal, liability, and supplemental unemployment benefit (SUB) insurance. Regardless of type or kind, actuaries are needed to make precise judgments regarding the financial impact of these plans. Several different approaches may be used. The company can set aside money each year to meet anticipated claims under a "self-insurance" plan. This approach should be used only with large numbers of employees and large corporate entities. The process can be risky and is most often found in public institutions (Henderson 1979). Commercial insurers can also be used. This is most often done through a bidding process or by individual contract arrangement in conjunction with skilled actuaries. Company-sponsored life insurance programs, which offer a modicum of financial stability for the family in the event of the death of the employee, can also be used.

For the most part, life insurance plans are offered as part of a group plan, which is able to offer the benefit of lower rates due to the fact that all employees are enrolled. The general guide businesses should follow is for the benefit to equal two years of the employee's total wages or salary.

Options to be considered include offering increased benefit dollars as the worker's tenure with the company increases and offering workers the opportunity to purchase added amounts at nominal fees and to purchase coverage for family dependents (Henderson 1979).

Coverage payment normally results in companies paying 100 percent of the premiums and workers paying for options. Other less frequent contribution splits range from 80 percent employer, 20 percent worker to 50–50 for each party.

According to Henderson (1979), standard life insurance features include total worker participation, with the health status of the individual not taken into account; conversion to an individual policy can be arranged if the worker decides to discontinue employment. This usually must take place within 30 days or some other specified time. Worker coverage may also be continued for 30 days upon leaving the company or upon retirement.

Bargaining over insurance benefits generally takes one of two courses. Either a defined set of benefits might be demanded by the union or a certain amount of money is to be allocated for certain benefits. In the case of a defined set of benefits, the management negotiator needs accurate long-term bids from insurance companies. Asking only one carrier could result in an inflated price as it cannot be assumed all insurance companies offer the same prices. In cases where a certain amount of money is to be allocated for certain benefits, caution must be used not to buy what appears to be the biggest bag of benefits for the fixed dollar without thorough investigation.

Exhibit 3.8 Total Annual Cost of Life Insurance Benefit

	Current cost of plan			Cost of plan with 10 percent increase	
Annual salary	Number of workers	Premium per month	Cost of plan to company	Number of workers	Total cost of plan
Under $15,000	70	6	$ 5,040	70	$ 5,049
$15,000–$18,000	100	7	8,400	0	0
18,001– 21,000	20	8	1,920	100	9,600
21,001– 24,000	0	9	0	20	2,160
24,001– 27,000	10	10	1,200	0	0
Over $27,000	0	11	0	10	1,320
Total	200		$16,560	200	$18,120

Benefits that are too small will result in poor employee relations now and demands for large increases in later contracts.

Exhibit 3.8 shows a method for costing life insurance plans. It assumes employee life insurance cost is not constant (assumed premium cost), but varies with the employee's wage level. This factor would necessitate that it be included in the roll-up or add-on cost figure discussed in Chapter 2.

The projected 10 percent wage increase will raise the cost to the company by $1,560 or from 3.9 to 4.3¢ per hour (see Exhibit 3.8). This occurs because the machinist, assemblers, and layout technicians will all move up a premium cost category as a result of the wage increase.

Example 3.8: Calculation for current cost plan.

$$\text{Cost/hour} = \frac{\$16{,}560}{416{,}000 \text{ hours}} = 3.9$$

Calculation for cost plan with 10 percent increase.

$$\text{Cost/hour} = \frac{\$18{,}120}{416{,}000 \text{ hours}} = 4.3$$

COSTING HEALTH INSURANCE

Hospitalization expense coverage is seen in 85 percent of labor contracts. Of this group, 31 percent use service plans like Blue Cross, 26 percent use private commercial carriers, 9 percent use health maintenance coverage, and 19 percent use other plans. Total cost of expenses is provided for in 81 percent of plans and 79 percent pay duration of illness for hospitalization benefits (BNA 1983).

Dependents are covered in 91 percent of plans, up from 75 percent in 1979. The coverage is equal in value to that of the employees. Ninety percent of plans provide for the employer to pay the full cost and the other 10 percent have both sharing the costs. Surgical coverage is as common as hospitalization coverage. Similarly, major medical is almost as common, specified in 74 percent of contracts (BNA 1983).

Health insurance benefits cover virtually all employees in the majority of companies, with most including major medical provisions

Table 3.5 Increases in Health Benefit Costs

	Year	Individual	Family
Office and management employees	1978	$25.16	$66.73
	1974	15.85	41.27
Nonoffice or management	1978	29.18	79.40
	1974	16.78	44.63

Source: Compiled from *Compensation Review*, "Compensation Currents . . . Benefits," American Management Association, 1979, p. 10.

as part of the package. The plans contain a limitless variety of assistance-type programs. A recent survey across industry groups reveals that dental plans are included in 41 percent of the contracts and 30 percent have prescription drug programs ("Compensation Currents . . ." 1979). The above survey shows that the cost of this service has increased over recent years (see Table 3.5). Its findings are supported by the survey work of Michael Granof (1973), who found the cost of accident and health insurance becoming a larger portion of labor cost. For example, in a recent *Wall Street Journal* article, it was reported that General Motors spent $3,270 on health benefits for each of its 522,000 employees in 1981. This figure reflects a 12 percent increase from 1980 and a 113 percent increase from the 1975 figure of $1,534 per employee. According to Henderson (1979), basic types of medical plans in the hospital and surgical area include:

1. Hospitalization plans offered by commercial insurance companies provide fixed cash benefits for hospital room and board plus other stated hospital costs. These plans can pay directly to the hospital or to the insured, who in turn pays the hospital. Blue Cross service plan systems are slightly different from commercial plans. They pay the hospital directly for room, board, and necessary hospital services in lieu of direct cash payments to the individual.
2. Expanded plans include diagnostic visits to the medical doctor's office and an annual physical.
3. Vision care and dental care benefits are important and popular additions to medical coverage to protect workers from the cost of these needed services.

Example 3.9 outlines a costing technique for health insurance. Assume the health insurance plan has a flat rate charge for each employee, which is the norm for such plans. To determine the total cost and cost per hour of the company portion of the expense, employee-funded portions (if any) need not be figured.

Example 3.9: Assume the following figures:

1. Plan fee of $35/month for each employee
2. 200 covered employees
3. Total cost of the plan

   200 X $35 X 12 months = $84,000

4. Cost per hour

$$\frac{\$84{,}000}{416{,}000 \text{ hours}} = 20.1¢ \text{ per hour}$$

This plan would cost $84,000 or 20¢ per hour to provide. However, since it does not vary with salary or wage level, it is not included in the add-on figure. It should, however, be added when discussing the total compensation package at the bargaining table or when communicating with employees about their total effective pay level.

Computing a union request for expanded coverage by adding to the plan or assuming a larger portion of the cost (that is, part of the employee contribution) is a simple process of multiplication.

Example 3.10:

1. Cost of the expanded coverage demand is $5 per month for each employee.
2. Additional cost

   $5 X 200 X 12 = $12,000

3. Cost per hour of change

$$\frac{\$12{,}000}{416{,}000 \text{ hours}} = 3¢$$

4. New total cost of package

   $84,000 + $12,000 = $96,000

5. New cost per hour of total package

$$\frac{\$96{,}000}{416{,}000 \text{ hours}} = 23¢$$

Another factor not included in this computation but which should be remembered is the total effect or "spillover" effect. Health insurance is provided to all employees, union and nonunion, as are most benefits. The above computations have focused on employees covered by the union contract. When introducing the model for figuring wages and benefits, it was mentioned there were 300 employees, 200 of whom were covered by the collective bargaining agreement. It is important to note that any benefit changes granted to the covered workers will also be given to those not included in the collective bargaining agreement. When figuring the cost of the agreement, be sure to compute any spillover effects for the other 100 workers. Spillover and its cost ramifications will be discussed in more detail in a later chapter, along with other factors of a similar nature.

COSTING SICK PAY

Most companies report a policy that allows employees to take time off for being sick without loss of job or pay. Most of these benefits are funded by the company up to a point, after which commercial insurance plans will often pick up the tab for extended absences.

Exhibit 3.9 Current and Projected Sick Pay

Job category	Number of workers	Pay rate	Number of days sick	Number of hours	Current cost per year	Pay rate w/10 percent increase	Projected total cost
Layout technician	10	$12	5	40	$ 480	$13.20	$ 528
Machinist	20	10	5	40	400	11.00	440
Assembler	100	8	45	360	2,880	8.80	3,168
Laborer	70	6	25	200	1,200	6.60	1,356
Total					$4,960		$5,492

Cost estimates for a sick leave plan are based on accurate record-keeping of the number of days sick by the various classifications of workers. A historical trend line is the best estimate possible for future demands, barring any new source of data for more accurate predictions. How generous the plan and whether there is any allowance for personal business leave will help figure the degree of usage. The accumulation of sick leave is a policy matter. Some companies allow sick leave to accumulate and be taken at retirement, although many companies put limits on the maximum number of days (100 is common) that can be carried at any given time.

Another factor that must be remembered is replacement cost for sick workers if such action is necessary for continued operation. Of course, any contemplated wage increases will increase the cost of this benefit. Paid sick leave is provided in 28 percent of contracts with 92 percent of these provisions calling for the regular pay rate (BNA 1983).

Example 3.11: Using figures from Exhibit 3.9:

Current cost/hour	Projected cost
$\frac{\$4{,}960}{416{,}000} = 1.1¢$	$\frac{\$5{,}492}{416{,}000} = 1.3¢$

Sick leave calculations are performed in Example 3.11. Assume that the contract allows for one sick day per month with an accumulation maximum of 100 days. A hypothetical number of sick days used is assumed. The example also assumes a 10 percent negotiated wage increase and projects the cost based on this increase. As is shown in Example 3.11 the cost with the projected increase is $5,492, or 1.3 cents per hour per year.

CAFETERIA-TYPE BENEFIT SELECTION

A rather new approach being used in some organizations is to allow employees to choose the benefits they wish to receive on an individual basis. From the cost analysis vantage point, these open choice situations enable the company to explain the cost and worth of individual benefit programs to employees. In theory, the employees have a pool of funds to spend on benefits, know the cost of each item purchased, and know how much money remains in the pool for added selection. The pool for that person is exhausted when benefit purchases use up the allotted funds.

Note, however, that some benefits (such as Social Security) are mandated by law. Benefits mandated by law and by contractual agreement with the union will reduce the pool of available funds for individual selection of benefits.

These flexible plans, often referred to as "cafeteria" plans, are said to accomplish four basic goals in a sound compensation program: they display a desire on the part of the employer to improve the employee's quality of life; enhance employee output; heighten employee awareness of the values and costs of benefits supplied by the organization; and add to employee understanding of the value and cost of total benefit programs (Henderson 1979).

Allowing individual choice can result in the organization's incurring higher costs. With all employees participating in each category, the cost of a benefit can be reduced. With reduced numbers participating by selecting other benefits, the cost may increase for some benefits.

There is no strong evidence to suggest that cafeteria plans are overwhelming successes. Because of high numbers of mandated and agreed-upon benefits, choice is reduced significantly. In these cases, the flexibility that allows the selection of benefits important to young workers (such as maternity) and older workers (pension) may be so slight as to be meaningless. Yet, selection options are on the increase. For example, 23 percent of hospitalization provisions in union contracts allow employees to choose between different types of coverage (BNA 1983).

Costing of benefits under a cafeteria-type flexible plan is the same as costing of benefits under any other plans. The main difference comes in the data collection and storage by the organization, where it may require more time and effort to track the individual differences.

TOTAL COST OF NEGOTIATED BENEFITS

Benefit costs accumulate quickly. The individual costs for some appear slight, only 1¢ or 3¢ per hour. Collectively, they can increase to between 30 and 40 percent of straight-time pay.

Not every possible economic benefit has been discussed. The principal ones were covered and a visible pattern of costing these

Exhibit 3.10 Negotiated Benefits

Benefit	Total current cost	Cost/hour (dollars)	Projected cost	Projected cost/hour (dollars)
Holiday pay	$123,200	.296	$155,948	.370
Vacation (straight-time replacement, not compression or an adjusted schedule)	185,440	.446	203,984	.490
Pension	320,320	.770	387,587	.930
Life insurance	16,560	.039	18,120	.043
Health insurance	84,000	.201	96,000	.230
Sick pay	4,960	.011	5,456	.013
Total	$734,480	$1.763	$867,095	$2.076

(and other similar benefits) becomes apparent. Benefits classified as economic by some may be classified as noneconomic to others. Jury duty, wash-up time, uniforms, company business, and paid lunch are some controversial benefits discussed in the next chapter.

How did the company fare in the examples used? Based on the six benefits discussed in a costing format, the increase was from $734,480 to $867,095 or an increase in total cost to the company of $132,615 (see Exhibit 3.10). In terms of cost per hour, this went from $1.763 to $2.076 per hour or an increase of 31.3¢ per hour (see Exhibit 3.10). This rather dramatic increase demands that the contract-costing analyst assess its impact on the overall profitability levels of the company. How this is done is the subject of Chapters 5 and 6.

STATUTORY BENEFITS

Obvious by their absence from the above examples are statutory insurance and other benefit coverage. Among the programs of this type are Social Security (old age, survivors', and disability insurance), workmen's compensation, unemployment, and disability insurance.

Because of the precise requirements set forth in those areas, most companies are aware of these costs. However, to be complete in costing the benefit package, these must be added because of their large cost. These costs now average 9 percent of payroll cost. The example will use figures close to current cost. The requirements for some of these benefits vary from state to state and the Social Security costs are ever increasing. It is hoped the percentages used will be representative. Even if they do change, as it is suspected they will, the format for computation will be the same.

If Exhibit 3.10 of negotiated benefits is revised to add the statutory requirements in Exhibit 3.11, the economic benefit package

Exhibit 3.11 Statutory Benefits

Social Security

9.2 percent of first $32,000 of wages (straight time, overtime, vacation, and holiday pay); all workers fit into this limit

9.2 percent X $3,203,200 (total = $294,694 payroll)

cost/hour = 70.8¢

State Unemployment Insurance

Assume contribution of 2 percent of the first $7,800 of wages for each employee

$7,800 X 200 employees X 2 percent = $31,200

cost/hour = 7.5¢

A 10 percent wage increase will have no effect since all employees made over $7,800

Workmen's Compensation

Assume a payment rate of 2 percent of total payroll cost, current cost

2 percent X $3,203,200 = $64,064

cost/hour = 15.4¢

With a 10 percent wage increase, the cost per hour and total cost figures change:

2 percent X $3,523,520 = $70,470

cost/hour = 16.9¢

Exhibit 3.12 Negotiated and Statutory Benefits

Benefit	Total current cost	Cost/hour	Projected cost	Projected cost/hour
Negotiated benefit from Exhibit 3.10	$734,480	$1.763	$867,095	$2.076
Social Security	294,694	.708	324,164	.779
State unemployment	31,200	.075	31,200	.075
Workmen's compensation	64,064	.154	70,470	.169
Total	$1,124,438	$2.70	$1,292,929	$3.099

begins to approach the national averages. Exhibit 3.12 shows that with negotiated and statutory benefits included, the cost per hour is slightly over $3.00 for the projected new contract.

SUMMARY

Chapter 3 approaches the topic of how to figure the cost of economic fringe benefits for employees. The introductory section examines how expensive these items have become to business. According to various surveys, costs range from $5,560 to $6,837 per employee per year. Costs have increased for many reasons, including tax advantages to both employee and company, and lack of awareness by managers as to the extent of benefits (including nonproductive time payments such as holidays and breaks).

Techniques for figuring the more commonly offered benefits are presented in a discussion on how to control the cost of certain benefit areas. The discussion also includes special efforts to alert the reader to often hidden costs of offering certain benefits. Hidden costs include such items as personnel processing time, benefits for replacement workers, training, and so forth.

In addition to voluntary benefit items, the chapter concludes with techniques to figure the cost of mandatory benefits such as unemployment insurance, Social Security, and other government-required coverage.

SKILL-BUILDING EXERCISE

Assume the following information about the company and compute answers to the questions that follow. Use replacement rates and cost factors.

a. Number of employees–500
b. Rate of pay (average)–$6.00/hour
c. Overtime rate–$9.00/hour
d. Paid time off
   1. ten days vacation after two years; 15 days after five years
   2. six holidays
   3. two personal leave days
e. Replacement ratio 74 percent
f. Replacement cost factor 10 percent
g. Last year's overtime average–150 hours per employee
h. Scheduled work year–52 weeks X 40 hours/week

1. What is the current straight-time payroll? What is the total payroll with overtime?

2. What is the cost per hour of the vacation benefit? (Assume 50 percent of the employees have over five years service.)

   a. What will the cost be in terms of total cost and cost per hour with the following union demands?

      1. 10 days immediate
      2. 15 days after two years
      3. 20 days after five years

3. What is the current cost of the holiday premiums? What is the cost if the union requests three added days?

4. What is the cost of the personal leave benefit? How will it change if two added days are agreed to?

5. What is the cost per hour of

   a. all current benefits
   b. proposed changes

   without using replacement ratio and cost factor adjustments?

4

Costing Noneconomic Benefits

INTRODUCTION

Most labor contracts have noneconomic clauses or clauses that address matters that appear to be incidental in nature. These clauses are perceived as having less financial impact than economic clauses, are primarily of a policy-setting nature, and address issues from the local union setting.

Frequently, these clauses result in important financial considerations. The perceived proportion of a new cost adjustment to overall labor cost is often not great. As a result, the item is dismissed as immaterial. A 1979 U.S. Chamber of Commerce survey indicated that these benefits can account for approximately 4 percent of total payroll cost.

Consider, for example, the impact of contract provisions relating to "work assignments." This area is considered noneconomic by most companies. But if changes occur that permit workers to have their own choice of job assignments using seniority as a basis, then management flexibility is limited. The company cannot assign the most qualified person to the job and efficiency declines.

Granof's findings showed that few companies attempt to take such points into account during negotiations. A job-bid system clause negotiated into a 1968 coal industry contract altered management prerogative in job assignments, which has had an impact on productivity. The exact extent to which productivity is affected has not been measured; however, coal industry managers are aware that the job-bid clause is not a noneconomic item (Holoviak 1980).

PAID LUNCH, REST PERIODS, AND WASH-UP TIME

Paid lunch, rest periods, and wash-up time are considered to be noneconomic benefits. Table 4.1 indicates the frequency of occurrence of each benefit in manufacturing and nonmanufacturing contracts.

A Bureau of National Affairs survey (1979) indicates that for agreements that specify the amount of lunch time granted, 66 percent are for 30 minutes and 23 percent for 60 minutes. However, in 17 percent of contracts, if an employee works through the scheduled lunch period, overtime pay provisions are provided.

Rest periods are approached from two perspectives. In 10 percent of the cases they are governed by past practice in the plant. In most cases they are governed by detailed contract provisions that specify when, how long, and how many rest periods are agreed to by the parties. The majority of contracts offer two rest periods per shift, with 50 percent allowing ten minutes and 40 percent allowing 15 minutes (BNA 1983).

Wash-up or clean-up time is mentioned in 22 percent of the contracts (BNA 1983). However, the terms used are general and can mean either actual personal cleaning or changing of clothes. The time specified is either five or ten minutes, with five being the more frequent.

Table 4.1 Frequency of Noneconomic Benefits

Benefit	Percent across all contracts	Percent manufacturing	Percent nonmanufacturing
Paid lunch	48	43	56
Rest periods	34	32	36
Wash-up time	20	22	16

Source: Compiled from Bureau of National Affairs (BNA), *Basic Patterns in Union Contracts* (Washington, D.C.: Bureau of National Affairs, 1979), pp. 30–32.

COSTING PAID LUNCH, REST, AND WASH-UP PROVISIONS

The cost of these contract provisions is simply the cost in dollars divided by the hours worked. The cost of a union request for a 30-minute paid lunch period for all covered workers is identified in Exhibit 4.1. A 50-week (250 working days) year is assumed; however, actual number of days worked should be used when known. Cost paid for a 30-minute lunch would then be \$192,500. To arrive at the cost per hour of this benefit, the dollar figure is divided by the number of hours worked. In this example, it would cost the company approximately 46¢ per hour to agree to the union request for the 200 employees covered.

Example 4.1:

$$\text{Cost/hour} = \frac{\text{Dollar cost benefit}}{\text{Hours worked}}$$

$$= \frac{\$192{,}500}{416{,}000} \quad (2{,}080 \text{ hours} \times 200 \text{ workers})$$

$$= 46.3¢$$

Example 4.1 shows the computation for the cost of two ten-minute rest periods for the covered workers as requested by the union, using information presented in Exhibit 4.2. Again the example

Exhibit 4.1 Cost of Paid Lunch

Job category	Pay rate per hour	Number of workers	Cost per day (½ hour rate × number of workers)	Cost per year (250 days)
Layout technician	\$12	10	\$ 60	\$ 15,000
Machinist	10	20	100	25,000
Assembler	8	100	400	100,000
Laborer	6	70	210	52,500
Total				\$192,500

Exhibit 4.2 Cost of Paid Rest Periods

Job category	Pay rate per hour	Number of workers	Cost per day (1/3 hour rate X number of workers)	Cost per year (250 days)
Layout technician	$12	10	$ 40	$ 10,000
Machinist	10	20	60	15,000
Assembler	8	100	240	$ 60,000
Laborer	6	70	126	31,500
Total				$116,500

assumes a 50-week working year or 250 working days. The cost of this demand is $116,500 and equals 28¢ per hour in that form of costing.

Example 4.2:

$$\text{Cost/hour} = \frac{\text{Cost benefit}}{\text{Hours worked}}$$

$$= \frac{\$116{,}500}{416{,}000 \text{ hours}} \text{ (2,080 hours} \times \text{200 workers)}$$

$$= 28.0¢$$

The wash-up time example assumes a five-minute clean-up period for all covered workers. This may not actually be the case since not all job categories would require clean-up or clothes change. However, assume that the five-minute period is either for clean-up or to change clothes for those who must wear special clothing. The cost of a union request for a five-minute clean-up/clothes change per Exhibit 4.3 is $32,250 annually. Note that the cost per hour figure is almost 8¢.

Exhibit 4.3 Cost of Wash-up Time

Job category	Pay rate per hour	Number of workers	Cost per day (1/12 hour rate × number of workers)	Cost per year (250 days)
Layout technician	$12	10	$10	$ 2,500
Machinist	10	20	17	4,250
Assembler	8	100	67	16,750
Laborer	6	70	35	8,750
Total				$32,250

Example 4.3:

$$\text{Cost/hour wash-up benefit} = \frac{\text{Cost}}{\text{Hours worked}} = \frac{\$32{,}250}{416{,}000 \text{ hours}} = 7.7¢$$

When paid lunch, rest periods, and wash-up time are considered together, the cost is substantial. The annual total amounts to $341,250. Most companies are, or should be, interested in the cost per hour of benefits; these three rather common benefits equal a cost of approximately 82¢ per hour.

Some additional comments are necessary to complete the discussion regarding these items. All three benefits were computed for only the employees covered by the union agreement. Yet, in the case of paid lunch and rest periods or breaks, the same benefits are given to other employees not covered by the agreements such as secretaries, staff workers, and nonexempt workers, thereby increasing the true cost of these items. This is referred to as a spillover effect and is covered in more detail in a later section.

In addition, there are instances in which it might be necessary to use overtime pay rates rather than straight-time pay rates. The assumption made when using straight-time pay rates is that workers' production capability is increased due to the above allowances for time away from the job; therefore, their production rate is not affected–they continue to produce 100 widgets a day. However, in some instances this is not true, and the production rate is lower. In these instances overtime hours may be needed to make up that lost production. These costs must be included in overall cost calculations.

PAID LEAVE FOR JURY DUTY

Figuring the cost of paid leave for jury duty is difficult. Precise figures are not readily available. The best technique is the use of the historical trendline: analysis of what it has cost in past years and the projection of these costs into the future. The cost per hour figure is computed as in the prior examples:

$$\text{Cost/hour} = \frac{\text{Total dollar cost to the company}}{\text{Number of hours worked}}$$

Leave to perform jury duty or other forms of court or civil responsibility is provided for in 83 percent of contracts. Payment is the employee's regular wage less any fee received. Thirteen percent of the contracts in the BNA sample did place limits on the number of paid jury leave days (BNA 1983).

BEREAVEMENT PAY

Paid leave for a death in the family is difficult to project in precise dollar terms. The best alternative is to use some form of historical index to estimate future costs. The number of contracts offering this benefit increased from 57 percent in 1971 to 80 percent in 1979 and to 82 percent in 1983. Of the contracts granting funeral leave, 90 percent give three days, with the remaining 10 percent offering between one and five days (BNA 1983).

Example 4.4 computes the cost of this benefit assuming levels of usage drawn from historical data presented in Exhibit 4.4. The benefit illustrated is three-days bereavement pay. The cost is $3,024 or less than 1¢ per hour to the company. Funeral leave is generally not an expensive item even when figuring replacement cost. This may explain its increased popularity as a benefit item.

Exhibit 4.4 Cost of Bereavement Pay Benefit

Job category	Pay rate	Number of workers who used provision	Number of days (3-day benefit per worker)	Number of hours (number of days × 8)	Total cost
Layout technician	$12	2	6	48	$ 576
Machinist	10	3	9	72	720
Assembler	8	6	18	144	1,152
Laborer	6	4	12	96	576
Total					$3,024

Example 4.4:

$$\text{Cost/hour} = \frac{\text{Total cost paid in benefit}}{\text{Number hours worked}}$$

$$= \frac{\$3{,}024}{416{,}000}$$

$$= .7¢$$

MEETINGS BETWEEN MANAGEMENT AND UNION LEADERS

Meetings between management and union leaders have become a popular mechanism for promoting effective communication between these groups. This area of interaction draws heavily from Japanese management models, particularly their quality circles. For example, 45 percent of labor contracts now call for safety-health committees, and union-management cooperative clauses are included in 37 percent of contracts, up from 12 percent in 1975 (BNA).

A program proposal to improve the quality of communication between management and labor has many farsighted benefits. On the other hand, these forums can be just ego trips for union and management leaders. Such programs will require committee members to be excused from their jobs to attend meetings, incurring costs for lost production time and possible travel expenses. In such cases, the demand should be reviewed carefully.

Various forms of committees are becoming popular and cost-benefit analysis should be instituted early to insure they are productive. Remember, some committee members may be performing critical jobs and may need to be replaced during the time spent in meetings.

Cost-benefit analysis should include a wide category of items to judge the effectiveness of the program. Some of the points to monitor include: changes on scrap or waste, reject rate, absenteeism, tardiness, customer returns, illness rates, output (productivity), changes in cost basis, and grievance rates.

Labor contract analysts need to monitor all elements in the cost benefit list, since it is common to see initial productivity decline when joint effort committees are utilized. Unfortunately, most of these current efforts will be more for show by both parties than genuine efforts to jointly increase productivity. It is particularly important to gather accurate costing data at contract expiration to substantiate party positions for the renewal contract.

UNION BUSINESS

Leave from work assignments to perform union duties exists in 85 percent of manufacturing contracts (BNA 1979). However, research by Granof found that few companies take the time to cost such proposals. Categories of union business typically include situations where a union officer is representing an employee to management and those areas that are strictly union business. Table 4.2 data show the results of a Bureau of Labor Statistics survey reflecting types of business for which union members are paid and the number of agreements that offer pay for each type of activity.

Customarily, stewards and officers process grievances on company time. In only 15 percent of all contracts is the number of hours paid to stewards for handling grievances limited. In just 22 percent of clauses the time is limited by vague terms, such as "unreasonable or excessive" (Bureau of Labor Statistics 1980).

Those firms that did evaluate the cost of contract changes involving union business computed it by taking the number of hours paid to stewards times their wage rates. Other cost estimates must be

Table 4.2 Paid Time for Union Business

Activity	Number of agreements paying for activity
All agreements*	1,550
Total referring to pay for time on union business	877
Grievance and/or arbitration	317
Contract negotiations	9
Other union business**	238
Grievance, arbitration, and contract negotiations	51
Grievance, arbitration, and other union business	171
Contract negotiations and other union business	8
Grievance, arbitration, negotiations, and other union business	36
Other***	47
No reference to pay for time on union business	673

*Includes agreements covering 1,000 workers or more, January 2, 1980.

**Other union business includes time spent collecting union dues, checking union cards, attending union conventions or training, attending labor-management committee meetings, and similar activities.

***Includes agreements that refer to no specific type of activity, that are unclear, or are subject to local negotiations.

Source: Bureau of Labor Statistics, Bulletin 2095, U.S. Department of Labor, Washington, D.C., 1980, p. 95.

added to arrive at a complete cost that will reflect leave for strictly union business plus the above. These include:

1. Cost of witness to testify at a grievance hearing;
2. Cost of salary for full-time union officers;
3. Cost of benefits for full-time union officers;
4. Cost of replacement for full-time union officers; and
5. Any possible estimate for lost productivity. (Granof 1973)

It is difficult for anyone to cost a union request worded in such vague terms as "reasonable" time and an "appropriate" or "sufficient" number of stewards to conduct business. Means by which this cost can be controlled include limiting the number of stewards through a contract clause or limiting the number of hours per a given time period that can be used for steward business. Clarification of these two points in the contract can aid in determining cost. In addition, past records regarding how many grievances were filed and how many conventions and other activities union delegates and officers attended will provide useful information.

It is not unusual for unions to request clauses in the contract providing for fully paid leave to attend both state and international union conventions. If five officers and delegates are excused for this strictly union business, 50 working days are lost for two one-week conventions. When premium pay must be granted to replace employees for 50 working days, the cost is not as immaterial as it is often perceived to be. Having these costs itemized and then computed as a cost per hour benefit applied to the contract package may prove to be a wise contract-costing strategy.

Example 4.5: Consider the following:

1. Five union stewards @ \$6.00 per hour
2. Allowed 20 hours per month union business
3. Five union officers and delegates attend two one-week conventions at full pay. Assume \$6.00 per hour and a 40-hour week
4. Replacement pay is issued at straight time for workers
5. 180 employees working 40 hours a week amounts to 374,400 hours worked

5 X 20 hours X \$6.00/hour	=	\$ 7,200 year
5 X 40 hours X \$6.00/hour X 2 conventions	=	2,400 year
5 X 80 hours X \$6.00/hour (replacement)	=	2,400 year
Total		\$12,000 year

$$\text{Cost/hour} = \frac{\text{Total cost of benefit}}{\text{Total hours worked}}$$

$$= \frac{\$12{,}000}{374{,}400}$$

$$= 3.2¢$$

Although 3¢ per hour is not a major factor in the cost of doing business, it must certainly be taken into account when figuring the benefits covered workers receive. The cash outlay here is $12,000 a year, which could be a sizable portion of a worker's pay. In addition, it should be noted that its cost is equal to or greater than some of the economic benefits.

WORKING CONDITIONS

At the beginning of this chapter there was some discussion as to how changes in working conditions may affect productivity and profits. Another example cited from *Costing Union Demands* (Heisel and Skinner 1976) may also serve to demonstrate this area of benefit costing.

> In a large public sector agency the union bargained for vacation schedules that permitted members to be granted summer vacations. Not an unusual request; however, the agency's peak work load activity was also in the summer. This clause made the employment of seasonal help as vacation replacements required. Now, instead of absorbing vacation cost during off-peak times or in lost productivity, it had to bear the expenses of added outlays for replacement workers. The cost of this clause to the agency included:
>
> 1. Salaries of temporary seasonal help;
> 2. Benefits available to them;
> 3. Any wage differentials paid to persons temporarily promoted;
> 4. Cost of employment processing;
> 5. Training cost of temporary and promoted replacements; and
> 6. Impact on productivity by having regular, more competent workers perform the job.

EMPLOYEE UNIFORMS

There is some debate as to the negotiability of uniform requirements or work clothes required for the job. Although there appears to be no specific National Labor Relations Board (NLRB) ruling that settles the issue, work clothes are considered to be different from safety clothes and equipment.

In 32 percent of labor contracts (up from 23 percent in 1979) this item can be found across all industry classifications, making an examination of specific industry patterns helpful. Provisions for work clothes or employee uniforms are found in 89 percent of retail contracts, 72 percent of services contracts, 72 percent of transportation contracts, 69 percent of chemicals contracts, 38 percent of food contracts, and 48 percent of construction contracts. Contracts that discuss uniforms require that they be supplied by the employer in 74 percent of the cases. In 51 percent of the cases the employer is responsible for cleaning and replacing the uniforms (BNA 1983).

There is an obvious economic cost impact to management of providing such a benefit on a unilateral basis. In addition, the union may insist on negotiating type and quality of uniforms, with a higher impact on contract cost than expected. A logical next step in negotiations would be for union leaders to request uniform maintenance subsidies, which could be quite costly.

Historical references can provide accurate primary cost data to compute this benefit in most situations. As in other benefits, this should be reduced to a cost per hour figure both to show employees and to enlighten management regarding the true cost of a labor agreement.

Example 4.6:

$$\text{Cost/hour} = \frac{\text{Cost of providing uniforms}}{\text{Total number of hours worked}}$$

TRAVEL EXPENSE REIMBURSEMENT

In 28 percent of contracts (up from 19 percent in 1979) travel necessitated by the job calls for expense reimbursement (BNA 1983). In the public sector, many agencies require employees to drive their own cars on public business. Their unions will negotiate a fixed mileage rate to compensate the employee.

According to the 1983 BNA survey, reimbursement for expenses away from headquarters are allowed for in 63 percent of contracts in the construction, transportation, and utility industries. Forty-one percent of contracts in the communications, retail, and utility industries allow for reimbursement for use of a personal car on company business. Thirty-five percent of contracts in the construction industry allow a daily allowance for travel; while 30 percent of contract travel clauses in the petroleum, printing, and transportation equipment industries allow reimbursement for moving and transfer expenses.

Heisel and Skinner (1976) note several good techniques for computation of the cost-of-travel reimbursement and suggestions for keeping track of those costs. Past records can be used to determine mileage paid and can be adjusted if increases are granted. Often these data are not kept in a central file, but a minor adjustment with accounting procedures can correct this. Possibilities for requiring alternate forms of transportation such as public transit or a car from a motor pool should be examined. A check should be made to see if any planned changes will require more travel than in the past. If so, this should be taken into account before going to the bargaining table.

UNEMPLOYMENT BENEFIT PROGRAMS

Supplemental Unemployment Benefit Plans

Although income security plans date back to the early 1920s, they were seldom negotiated at the bargaining table until the mid 1950s. Supplemental Unemployment Benefit (SUB) plans are designed to provide workers with financial protection against job layoff.

The company pays an agreed amount (such as 7¢ per hour worked) into a SUB fund for each paid labor hour. The funds are used to supplement unemployment compensation for laid-off workers. The employee's contribution to the fund is limited. These limits are negotiated and are often stated as an overall dollar value for the fund. Supplemental unemployment benefits are divided into pooled and individual account plans. Pooled fund methods provide for pay only in the event of lack of work and are the most common plans. Individual account plans provide workers vested rights to the account and may be withdrawn in full at termination. Due to the infrequency of individual accounts, discussion will center around pooled funds.

Most plans pay a percentage of the employees' straight-pay rate, which is added to the employees' unemployment compensation. This can equal 95 percent of take-home pay. Other plans vary from 60 to 85 percent of compensation. Note that certain groups (such as the Ladies' Garment Workers) pay a set lump-sum benefit per week.

Employer's liability is limited to the amount in the fund. When the fund is exhausted, no further liability exists. Therefore, forecasting costs in this area becomes a simple matter of projection of the agreed-to per hour contribution up to the fund's limit.

Again, in this area, breaking down the cost into a per hour figure may be helpful at negotiation time. Few companies bother even to include this item when reporting benefits to workers.

As will be discussed later, there is a possibility management could use these for collateral for loans or to satisfy bank deposit requirements. This reduces the opportunity cost to the employer for a possibly large pool of money. Of course, details regarding use of these funds must be agreed to in the labor contract.

Government Unemployment Programs

In most areas of the country, both private and public sector employees are covered by unemployment insurance. (The costing techniques for these were included in the discussion of mandatory benefit items.) Between state and federal programs, some employees have received benefits for as long as 65 weeks (Henderson 1979). The goal of most companies is to reduce their required contribution to the state unemployment compensation fund through stable work scheduling. The employer is required to pay both federal and state premiums or employer insurance tax. For state levels, the amount varies with each state.

Severance Pay

Another employment security program is severance pay. Severance pay plans are present in 45 percent of manufacturing and 28 percent of nonmanufacturing contracts (BNA 1983). Many of the severance pay plans are tied into SUB plan provisions. After a stated length of time on layoff with no prospect for recall, a company may elect to issue severance pay to a worker. SUB plan benefits would then cease. A minority (15 percent) of the plans also provides severance for workers who are ineligible for pension benefits.

The benefit amount is normally tied into a ratio of employee length of service. The amount ranges from one to 52 weeks. One week's pay for each year of service is the most frequently used ratio. The next most frequent is one-half week's pay for each year of service. Only 8 percent in the BNA survey of contracts paid a flat

Exhibit 4.5 Costing Severance Pay Plans

Job category	Weekly pay rate	Number terminated	Assumed current benefit eligibility	Current cost	Pay rate with 10 percent increase	Requested benefit eligibility	Total cost
Layout technician	$480	0	–	–	–	–	–
Machinist	400	0	–	–	–	–	–
Assembler	320	5	23 weeks	$7,360	$352	46	$16,192
Laborer	240	4	16 weeks	3,840	264	32	8,448
Total							$24,640

weekly amount for each year of service. Generally, a service requirement is stipulated for eligibility.

Nine percent of contracts require six months of service to be eligible for severance pay. Ten percent require five years of service, 13 percent require two, 15 percent require three, and 50 percent require only one year of service (BNA 1983).

Costing the severance pay benefit in the absence of any supporting data is usually done by investigating historical trends or assuming that last year's record will be similar to next year's. Information regarding certain economic and production forecasts should also be used in computing these costs. These could offer more insight into areas where terminations will take place.

Example 4.7 will assume a current benefit of one-half week's pay for each year of service for terminated employees. The maximum benefit amount is 26 weeks. Certain levels of service will be assumed in Exhibit 4.5. The union demands the benefit be increased to one week for each year and a 10 percent pay increase. This would result in a dramatic increase in cost to the company. Total dollar cost as shown in Exhibit 4.5 has increased from less than 3¢ to almost 6¢.

Example 4.7: Cost per hour under current benefit levels

$$\text{Cost/hour} = \frac{\$11{,}200}{416{,}000} \quad \text{(200 workers} \times \text{2,080 hours worked each year)}$$

Cost per hour with changes requested by union

$$\text{Cost/hour} = \frac{\$24{,}640}{416{,}000}$$

$$= 5.9¢$$

CAFETERIA BENEFIT

Employee dining facilities and benefits range from benches and vending machines to elaborate dining facilities. Often this service is a nonprofit operation and food may even be offered at below-cost prices with the company absorbing the losses.

Costing this benefit follows the traditional pattern. Attention should be made to include in the cost of total payments to concessionaires all fees paid, wages for people who work in dining facilities, cost of equipment, and any direct loss on food the company assumes. The formula for cost per hour is the familiar configuration used earlier.

Example 4.8:

$$\text{Cost per hour} = \frac{\text{Total cost to company for cafeteria}}{\text{Total hours worked}}$$

OTHER BENEFITS AND SERVICES

There is an increasing array of benefits and services that union and management negotiators have agreed to in recent years. The obvious goal from the management perspective is enhanced employee welfare and a stronger commitment to the goals of the organization. For the union negotiators, the services are valued by their members and offer the advantage of being easier to secure in recent years than larger wage increases.

As indicated earlier, there is little evidence to suggest companies are taking the necessary effort to compute the cost of these benefits as part of the total contract package. Many benefits are considered noneconomic in nature and may be difficult to arrive at a dollar value. However, the effort is necessary if the true total cost picture of a contract is to be determined.

According to Henderson (1979), benefits and services under this category can include:

1. Thrift or short-term savings plans
2. Stock purchase plans
3. Credit unions
4. Length of service awards and seniority awards
5. Referral awards
6. Christmas bonuses
7. Merchandise-purchasing plans
8. Charter flights and tours
9. Educational opportunities and subsidies
10. Gift matching
11. Social and recreational activities
12. Counseling
13. Legal services
14. Emergency loans
15. Moving and/or transfer allowances
16. Auto insurance
17. Umbrella liability coverage
18. Transportation and parking
19. Child adoption
20. Child care
21. Purchase of used equipment

Techniques used to cost this group of benefits are similar to those suggested for costing cafeteria food benefits. An effort should be made to include all aspects of company cost or losses absorbed. The cost-per-hour computation follows the format used throughout this chapter.

SUMMARY

This chapter presents an array of items that are frequently looked upon as noneconomic in nature and discusses how to cost them. Noneconomic benefits seldom receive the attention that more traditional items receive, primarily because they are seen as representing a very small cost. Taken separately, they are inexpensive when compared to individual economic items, but when considered as a whole they can add up to a substantial cost. The total dollar outlay represented in just the five examples in this chapter was $368,914, which amounts to almost 89¢ per hour per employee.

Problems discussed in the chapter with noneconomic benefits go beyond just the small expense of each item and the lack of management attention because of this. As indicated in survey findings, few companies take into account such items as job assignments and productivity impact due to changes in nonproductive work time.

SKILL-BUILDING EXERCISE

Assume the following information about company X and compute the answers to the questions that follow:

a. Number of employees–500
b. Average rate of pay–$3.00/hour
c. Overtime rate–$4.50/hour
d. Paid time off

    1. ten days vacation
    2. six holidays
    3. two personal leave days

e. Replacement ratio for workers–60 percent
f. Replacement cost factor–10 percent
g. Overtime–150 hours per employee per year
h. Scheduled work year–52 weeks × 40 hours per week

1. Figure the cost of the current 30-minute paid lunch break, total dollar and cost per hour.

    a. What would the cost be if the union requested a 60-minute paid lunch?

2. Compute the cost of a union demand for

    a. Two 10-minute breaks per shift
    b. One 5-minute wash-up period
    c. Figure total dollar and cost per hour at straight time and overtime. (Caution: Workers already average 150 hours overtime–how will this be affected?)

3. What is the best way to figure future cost for jury duty and bereavement pay? What is the cost of this benefit?

4. The union is demanding a uniform benefit. The cost of an average uniform is $100. The union wants every employee to have uniforms; management feels only 20 percent may need them. Compute both factors.

5. The union wants a SUB pay plan instituted. The plan would pay 7¢ for each hour worked per employee. What is the yearly liability to the company for the next three years, assuming no layoffs? The company wishes a $200,000 ceiling; when and will this affect future contract cost?

6. Severance pay is currently one week for each year of service. The union wishes this to be 1.5 weeks. Use the following schedule to judge the current cost of the benefit and the cost of the change:

   100 workers–20 years service–2 terminated
   300 workers–15 years service–5 terminated
   100 workers– 5 years service–1 terminated

5

Financial Analysis for Labor Negotiations

INTRODUCTION

The purpose of this chapter is to acquaint those involved in the labor relations process with the necessary skills for handling financial information. Both labor negotiators and management industrial relations people need to understand these skills.

Survey work in this field shows that the primary responsibility for management's collective bargaining has traditionally been in control of the industrial relations department. Accountants and financial analysts have been involved in the process in varying degrees; however, any large degree of involvement has been the exception rather than the rule. When one considers that relatively small changes in labor cost can produce large changes in profits, having the essential skills to evaluate financial impact becomes especially important.

Labor is also finding it necessary to sharpen the skills of its negotiators to ensure that negotiations result in reasonable demands. In an era of declining productivity coupled with inflation, increased costs, and heavy competition from foreign sources, the ramification of not doing so is loss of jobs for the union's constituency. Larger unions and medium and smaller bargaining units alike must provide a certain level of support in ensuring that financial analysis skills, which are crucial to successful negotiations, are developed at all levels.

CORPORATE STATEMENTS AND RELATED DATA

The Balance Sheet

A balance sheet can be defined as a financial picture of a company on one particular day. The left side of the picture shows assets, while the right side shows the liabilities and stockholders' equity. Both sides are always equal, or "balanced." Assets are typically the goods and property of the company and claims against other parties that have not yet been received. Liabilities are the debts due on behalf of the company.

Early research work reveals that union leaders have seldom utilized balance sheet data. The assumption has been that if the company is profitable, it automatically has the cash to pay wage and benefit demands. Income statement analysis is what has been used to gather the information regarding profitability.

A balance sheet is a tool that can be used to identify critical factors that impact on company profitability. Investigation and understanding of these factors can, in many instances, contribute toward gaining a more realistic picture of the company's ability to pay than could be obtained by looking at the income statement alone. Parts of the balance sheet that are particularly important to consider in the analysis are fixed assets, inventory, and retained earnings.

Fixed assets are among the most important factors to be considered in deciding the company's true ability to pay. A figure for depreciation is usually reported in relation to the fixed asset figure. Interpretation of the depreciation figure can be quite complex and often produces misleading results. Many people mistakenly assume that "money" amounts recorded as depreciation are set aside and available for use. This is rarely the case. This figure, rather, reflects the amount of money management might need to pull out of its cash flow to replace a machine.

Note also that the method of depreciation used by management affects the profitability reported on the income statement. Accelerated depreciation, for example, would tend to understate profitability.

Inventory figures should be carefully considered. Not only can they help in identifying the company's ability to pay, but they can also be used to identify changes that might be on the horizon that will affect the employment picture.

Changes in inventory levels might signal several different possibilities. If, for instance, production is maintained at the same level and inventories are increasing, one of several things might be happening. Sales could be falling, which could result in layoffs in the future. Junk inventories might be padding the figure, which could indicate problems in planning or quality control. On the other hand, legitimate build-up could signal that management is setting up a situation that would position the company to hold out on negotiation issues, even to the point of strike, without suffering a huge loss of income from lost sales.

Inventory costing is a complex process and varies from company to company. To get a true picture of what the inventory figure means on both the balance sheet and the income statement, the method of costing or "valuation" must be understood. It affects not only the inventory-cost figure but also the cost-of-goods-sold figure. The method of valuation tends to be chosen with respect to how it will affect the tax picture of the firm as reflected on the income statement. Without looking at the balance sheet and the income statement and considering the valuation method, one cannot obtain a true picture. There are three main methods of valuation: average cost, first-in-first-out, and last-in-first-out.

Average cost represents the average cost of all inventory items. This method has not been widely used in the past, due to the fact that computation on a day-to-day basis was perceived as being prohibitively cumbersome. It does, however, present the truest costing option and, with the advent of the computer era, will probably enjoy more widespread use.

First-in-first-out or historical valuation (most commonly referred to as FIFO) will result in the highest level of current income on the income statement and the highest stated inventory on the balance sheet. FIFO can, therefore, overstate the level of internal financing implied by the net income figure.

Last-in-first-out (most commonly referred to as LIFO) valuation will result in the lowest level of current income on the income statement and the lowest level of stated income on the balance sheet.

Retained earnings should be examined carefully. The source, nature, and destination of the reserves should be scrupulously examined. Unions indicate that failure to explain contingency reserves results in undue suspicions as to management intentions. An explanation that the reserve is not going to improperly take away from an

Exhibit 5.1 Balance Sheet

Assets

Current Assets

Consists of cash and other assets that will be converted into cash in the near future, usually within one year. Current assets include:

Cash

Bills, silver, petty cash, and money on deposit in the bank.

Marketable Securities

Temporary investment of excess or idle cash that is not immediately needed.

Accounts Receivable

Funds not yet collected from customers for goods shipped.

Inventories

Inventories for manufacturers consist of raw materials for use in manufacture, partially finished goods, and finished products ready for shipment.

Prepaid Current Expenses

Those expenses due in the short term that are paid in advance or are part of a larger payment attributed to this period.

Fixed Assets

Normally refers to property, plant, and equipment of the company. These assets are used continually by the company to produce the product and are not for sale to customers in the ordinary course of business. Includes such items as land, buildings, machinery, and office equipment. In addition, there is a figure for depreciation. The generally accepted method for valuation of assets is net of this accumulated figure.

Depreciation

This is often defined in accounting texts as the decline in useful value from use and time. However, decline in value may result from obsolescence as well as use. The decline in value may be used by management negotiators to support arguments for setting aside funds to replace obsolete equipment.

Intangibles

These assets may have no real physical presence, yet have value to the company. Intangibles include assets such as patents (if purchased), franchises, and goodwill. All costs involved in developing the product/process are usually expensed in the year incurred.

Liabilities

Current Liabilities

This tends to designate short-term obligations. These items have entered the balance sheet as a result of acquisition of materials and supplies used to make the product.

Accounts Payable

Amount the company owes its regular creditors. This area typically includes supplies when raw materials and supplies are bought on open account.

Notes Payable

Money owed to a bank or other lender in the short term.

Accrued Expenses

This typically includes such items as wages owed employees, insurance premiums, attorney fees, interest on loans, and similar expenses.

Federal Income Tax

By virtue of its amount and impact on the company, this expense item owed is normally listed separately. Many companies have a liability called "deferred income taxes" in addition to taxes listed in this section. Most larger companies will use a different method of accounting for tax purposes than for financial statement purposes. Companies could show a loss on their tax return while showing a profit on their financial statements. In effect, there are two sets of books kept: one for the IRS and one for shareholders, banks, employees, and the like. This is all legal. Deferred taxes come from the difference in the taxable income due to the difference in the two methods used. In practice, this "liability" will never be paid.

Long-Term Liabilities

These are debts due by the company with time periods in excess of one year.

Stockholders' Equity

This typically consists of the total equity interest invested by stockholders in the company and is divided into three areas.

Capital Stock

In a general definition, this is the proprietary interest in the company represented by stock certificates issued by the company. The division is generally between common and preferred stock.

(continued)

Exhibit 5.1 (continued)

Capital Surplus

The amount paid by shareholders that is in excess of the stated or par value of the stock. Currently, many companies issue stock without a par value, in which case no such entry would exist under this category.

Accumulated Retained Earnings

This is often called "earned surplus," and represents the retained portion of current and prior years' net income, plus or minus nonrecurring gains or losses, credits, charges, and similar items tied directly to retained earnings. Under certain circumstances, this may be transferred to other accounts within the stockholders' equity category.

income account entry will relieve union suspicion. The various particulars of the balance sheet that remain will be discussed in conjunction to their use in ratio analysis.

Other items that are important to consider include the fact that many companies offer warranties. They will have an account in the liability section of their balance sheet called "Reserve for Future Warranty Costs." This account is a requirement of generally accepted accounting principles (GAAP). For the contract negotiation analyst, this means there is a deduction on the income statement but no cash is spent. In later years the cash will be spent, but the company will get no deduction. Therefore, net profit will not be the same as cash.

Exhibit 5.1 takes a typical balance sheet format and describes each of the entry categories. There are no numbers used in the example; however, definitions and explanations are provided for contract analysts or negotiators not familiar with accounting. In a later section of this chapter references will be made to both balance sheet and income statement notations regarding their use in ratio analysis. Industry ratios, which can be used for comparison of individual organization ratios with the appropriate industry norm, are presented in the Appendix.

The Income Statement

The income statement shows how much the company makes or loses during the year and can provide much helpful information for use in labor negotiations. As in the case of assessing balance sheet information, income statement data can be adjusted to show labor and management capital shares and figures that can be taken out for closer scrutiny in ratio analysis.

The income statement spells out in precise form what has happened to income received from the selling of goods. Items commonly included are cost of goods sold, overhead expenses such as wages and salaries, rent, supplies, depreciation, interest on money borrowed, and taxes. The income statement shows the returns from operations realized by employees, creditors, government, stockholders, and the company. Note that inflation could result in the income statement showing a profit and increased sales, while there is actually a loss in constant dollars. It should also be kept in mind that profits are not idle cash waiting to be spent. These funds may be invested in plant, new computers, or other assets over long time periods. A short explanation of cash flows will save much time and effort for both parties in judging availability of money for wage and benefit increases.

There are two areas of difficulty in the use of the income statement. First, it often places too much emphasis upon the net earnings figure, which has the effect of downplaying other results. Second, payment to those who benefit from the enterprise are often either obscured or scattered in the statement, making viable comparison difficult at best.

A couple of examples may help clarify the above difficulties. First, a charge to labor may be treated as a charge for another commodity or service. The identity of the charge would then be lost in accounting distributions and classifications systems. In addition, depreciation on historical cost could result in profit being higher than it should be. The general purpose of depreciation is to provide a reserve for replacement. Therefore, depreciation based on historical cost does not always give a true picture, because inflation might have raised the cost of replacement. A specific example of this involves two companies that are exactly the same in all respects except that one just purchased a building for $1 million and the other has a building worth $1 million that was purchased 20 years ago for $100,000. Assuming no debt on either building, the income statement will be different for these companies. The company that just purchased the building will have a lower profit. The reason for the low profit figure is the depreciation for the latter is based on the $100,000 purchase and, after 20 years, there is little building value left to charge against

Exhibit 5.2 Income Statement

Gross Sales

Less Sales Returns

Sales returns are an important item and can be used as a labor relations tool. If returns are increasing as a percentage of gross sales, it could be an indicator of quality problems from labor's viewpoint or a management-control area.

Less Sales Discounts

This item in its net figure is the primary source of revenue for the company. If the company is other than a manufacturer, the term may be "operating revenue."

Cost of Goods Sold (Manufactured)

May be referred to as operating expenses. Represents all direct costs incurred in the process of producing the final product for sale. These costs include raw materials, labor, rent, electricity, supplies, and maintenance. Depreciation, administrative salaries, rent, advertising, and other fees are also listed in this group as a separate item, often called "general and administrative expenses."

Operating Profit

Subtracting all costs from net sales results in the operating profit figure.

Other Income

This figure is typically from dividends on interest from investments and can also be referred to as "miscellaneous income."

Total Income

This is the combination of operating profit and other income figures.

Interest Expense

Interest is paid to bondholders as part of the contractual agreement for use of their money. This is required regardless of company profitability. Dividends are only an obligation if the board of directors declares such.

Income Before Taxes

Federal Income Tax

The above are combined since what federal taxes are is of no mystery, but the typical presentation of income statements follows this arrangement.

Net Income (Net Profit)

After all income or revenue sources have been taken into consideration and all costs and expenses subtracted, the net income figure is the result.

---

for tax purposes. On the other hand, the new building will use accelerated depreciation for the $1 million purchase price. The resultant first year write-off could be in the neighborhood of $100,000. Each company should be considered equal in labor negotiations. "Equal" means the labor contract analyst or negotiator should be aware of such differences and make the necessary adjustments to depict the true profit levels of the company that recently purchased the building.

It has been offered that charges and credits to retained earnings should be used to compute financial statements for collective bargaining and negotiation purposes. This would mean all charges, credits, and tax transactions from which the company should not profit nor receive any negative feedback would be better located in a statement of retained earnings. The rationale offered for this is that an all-inclusive income statement can include items applicable to productive and fortuitous happenstance over the time period and may bear no direct relation to current period operations. It would be unreasonable for labor to enjoy windfall gains due to happenstance or to suffer penalties from events not connected to the productive operations in which they are a part (Pillsbury 1954).

As in the case for Exhibit 5.1, which presents the balance sheet, Exhibit 5.2 presents the income statement in generic terms. Descriptions and explanations of the income statement categories generally found are presented.

SINGLE-YEAR VERSUS MULTIYEAR ANALYSIS

Financial statements and relevant information for several years should be gathered for comparisons. In addition, a negotiator may wish to extrapolate the data to identify possible trends to develop a five-year outlook. Investment analysts in the stock market use a ten-year horizon. Analysis for a single year cannot be assumed to be typical of company activities over a longer period. Using statements over a longer period allows both union and management negotiators a much more realistic view of such trends. If the contract to be negotiated is for a three-year period, annual data are sufficient in lieu of monthly or quarterly breakdown of all the statements.

Union negotiators are advised to break down financial data they are using by plant or subsidiary companies. The nature of the bargaining units dictates to what extent the data need to be broken down. That is, if bargaining is done by individual units of a holding company, then data are needed for each unit. In a later section the question of information sharing and legal requirements are discussed. If, however, bargaining is on a companywide basis, such as in the auto industry, then as complete a breakdown is not necessary. In these cases, detailed data are necessary only for local issues. Management negotiators are aware that when unions request data on a detailed basis by individual units when bargaining is companywide, they are probably building a case for a special agreement.

USE OF RATIO ANALYSIS IN COLLECTIVE BARGAINING

Absolute dollar amounts and related data are certainly important in cost calculation to be used in the negotiation process. However, there are many limitations to its potential as a viable tool in this process. Ratio analysis is an invaluable aid in overcoming these limitations. Many of the following basic descriptions of ratios will be helpful to both management and union negotiating teams, while there are those that may be of particular interest to only one party. Note that ratios for individual firms should be compared to industrywide ratios. While there is generally an approximate minimum criterion for establishing the financial situation of a firm, comparison will give the negotiator a better picture of what is really happening. Appendix B expands on ratios for selected industries and provides definitions of standard terms.

Liquidity Ratios

There are several important ratios that can be derived from data given in the balance sheet. These are the net working capital, the current ratio, acid-test or quick-asset ratio, and total asset ratio.

Net working capital is the difference between total current assets and total current liabilities, and is a measure of short-term solvency. If working capital has increased between two periods, this can be a positive sign of profitable operations. However, the working capital position may have been improved by converting a portion of current liabilities into long-term debt. This case can be identified because certain other equity ratios will not show improvement between the two periods. Both sides of the negotiating position must consider the question of what would happen if working capital were to become significantly impaired. It is possible for both parties to receive some indication as to the impact of contract demands on working capital by conducting an analysis of the proposals on the affected items. Note that this should be done after the balance sheet and income statement have been adjusted to reflect proposed changes. Implied in this exercise are certain assumptions regarding sales level projections and other operational projections for the upcoming period that must also be integrated into this process.

The current ratio is found by dividing current assets by current liabilities. These figures are found on the balance sheet and are described in Exhibit 5.1. This ratio represents the extent to which current assets can cover short-term debt. While there are numerous exceptions, the minimum level of safety is believed to be a ratio of \$2 of current assets for every \$1 of current liabilities. Some believe this should be as high as \$3 to \$1. Current ratios for selected industries are presented in Table 5.1. Note that none of the ratios approaches the 3 to 1 mark, while some are close to 2 to 1. Also note that the current ratio may fluctuate during the year. Analysis of data from several years will establish a trend that will allow the negotiating team to judge the normal current ratio maintained by the company.

Labor negotiators attribute a great deal of significance to the acid-test or quick-asset ratio. The level of wages and benefits that can

Table 5.1 Average Industry Current Ratios

Industry	Current ratio
General construction	1.4
Food stores	1.5
Hotels	1.1
Auto manufacturers	1.8
Railroad	0.9
Retail stores	1.9

Source: Compiled from *Almanac of Business and Industrial Financial Ratios*, 1980, pp. 23, 182, 243, 313.

Table 5.2 Average Industry Quick Ratios

Industry	Quick ratio
General construction	0.7
Food stores	0.4
Hotels	0.8
Auto manufacturers	1.3
Railroads	0.5
Retail stores	0.8

Source: Compiled from *Almanac of Business and Industrial Financial Ratios*, 1980, pp. 23, 182, 243, 261, 313.

reasonably be requested by and granted to workers depends not only on the level of working capital, but also the relationship between "quick" or relatively liquid assets and current liabilities. This ratio is found by dividing current assets by current liabilities. Quick current assets are current assets minus inventories and usually include cash, temporary investments, and receivables. Figures for this calculation are found on the balance sheet and are described in Exhibit 5.1. Note that temporary investments should be included only if they can be disposed of without hampering the operations of the business and if there is a viable market with sufficient trading activity to yield a reasonable price. The rule-of-thumb is that a quick-asset ratio should be at least 1 to 1 in order to reflect a financially well-situated industrial company, that is, $1 of quick current assets to $1 of current liabilities. Table 5.2 presents selected industry ratios. Labor negotiators should take care to examine such things as whether cash required for payment of operating expenses or other similar items coincides with the due dates of receivables. Note, in addition, that even the rule-of-thumb of a 1 to 1 ratio is not positive proof of adequate liquidity to justify strong statements or demands.

The total asset ratio measures the relative financial strength of the company and indicates the pressure of long-term debt. Thus, as a proxy for long-term solvency, it takes into account debt increases relative to monies supplied by stockholders. As the debt level increases relative to shareholder monies, the company tends to be more dependent on its creditors for working capital. This form of leverage can make the organization subject to a crisis situation in the advent of a decline in the level of sales. The total asset ratio is found by dividing total capital by total assets. These figures are found on the balance sheet and are described in Exhibit 5.1. The larger the ratio of total capital to total assets is, the stronger is the financial position of the company. For labor negotiators, a large demand when this ratio is low and declining could force the company into insolvency in the event of a sales decline. On the other hand, careful attention to this ratio can serve as a basis for feeling a demand is reasonable in view of a strong financial condition and positive sales forecast.

Inventory Ratios

Inventory analysis represents an area of difficulty fraught with both theoretical and practical problems. Accountants seem, by and large, to have these problems pretty well under control in that they tend to agree on such things as methods of inventory valuation. Unfortunately, this is not true in the collective bargaining arena.

Division of thought dates back somewhat in time. For instance, Wilbur Pillsbury reported in 1954 that, for the most part, labor union officials were against LIFO methods of inventory valuation. For that matter, he reported, they were against any method other than using actual historical cost or FIFO in depreciating fixed assets. In the current inflationary environment, FIFO can result in windfall profits that would seem to benefit union negotiation positions. This is not to say unions and labor organizations are against LIFO or accelerated depreciation or any particular technique used for tax purposes. Instead, they call for careful use of these accounting tools in the preparation of financial statements for the collective bargaining process.

Accountants as a rule do not select an inventory depreciation method to confuse negotiators or stockholders or to hide money from the various tax agencies. Inventory that is sold needs to be replaced, and machinery and other fixed assets wear out. There are legitimate reasons to select a particular accounting method that will best reflect the company's financial position.

Generally, inventory management for manufacturers and the consequent need for funds is dependent on consideration of the situation in three areas: raw materials, work in progress, and finished goods. For wholesalers and retailers, inventory management deals usually with purchased goods. In addition, manufacturers, wholesalers, and retailers alike are constantly working to determine the optimal level for inventory stocks. Their considerations must include the volume of "safety" stock needed to avoid a stockout position, considerations for economy purchases, projected movement of the price of materials, the effects of volume usage, cost to carry inventory, and the availability and cost of funds to invest in inventory. There are many risks inherent in the inventory process. One is the possibility of price increases or decreases in raw materials. Obsolescence and deterioration of inventories present the company with added risks, as will any miscalculation of the level of investment in inventory as it relates to changes in sales volume. Other risks can include changes in market strategy; for example, some grocery stores are converting their inventory to fast-moving items only.

There are four primary inventory ratios of interest to negotiating teams. Inventory as a percent of sales or cost of sales is the first ratio to consider. This is calculated by dividing the inventory by the sales. These figures are found on the balance sheet and the income statement and are described in Exhibits 5.1 and 5.2.

The average number of days in inventory should also be calculated. This is a two-step process, the first step of which is to divide sales by 365 to find the average daily sales. This figure is then divided into the inventory to find the average number of daily sales in inventory.

Table 5.3 Inventory Turnover Ratios

Industry	Turnover ratio
Food stores	13.2
Auto manufacturers	6.6
Retail stores	4.6

Source: Compiled from *Almanac of Business and Industrial Financial Ratios*, 1980, pp. 23, 182, 243, 261, 313.

Inventory turnover, which records the movement of goods, can be calculated by dividing the cost of sales by inventory at cost. Table 5.3 shows selected industry turnover ratios.

A closely associated ratio that has direct ramifications for the extent of working capital available is the number of days of outstanding sales tied up in receivables. Here a comparison of average day's sales is divided into accounts receivable.

Comparisons should be made using accounting periods to insure comparability of data; do not compare a peak sales quarter (such as Christmas) to a slower spring quarter sales. It is important to mention that these figures are more meaningful when examined over a period of years rather than considered on a one-year basis.

RATIOS TO USE IN THE MANAGEMENT OF MONEY

An increase in profits is not sufficient evidence on which to base a wage increase request. The reason for the increase must be identified before a judgment can be made as to the reasonableness of the demand. It can be due to greater sales, increased margins, higher gross margins over the cost of goods sold, or operating expenses not increasing as much relative to sales.

One measure used to judge profitability is the relationship between net income after taxes and net sales. Net income after taxes is divided by net sales, giving the percent of net income attributable to sales. These figures are found on the income statement and are described in Exhibit 5.2. If the current ratio figure is lower than the past year's and current sales are higher, it can be assumed the company is not taking into its net profit a higher percent of revenues from sales, and therefore has correspondingly lower margins. For example, many businesses, in trying to keep the selling price of their product down, will merely pass on any price increases received. By doing so, the sales, cost of sales, gross profit, and net income will increase by an identical amount, but the percentage of net income to net sales will decrease.

One might also be interested in discovering the possible source of any difference in various expenses from year to year. An expense-to-sales ratio can be developed from figures from the income statement data, which are discussed in Exhibit 5.2. Appropriate dollar figures for the past three years for each category (such as cost of goods sold) are gathered from the income statement and divided by the sales figure. Example 5.1 outlines a format for analyzing these trends. The appropriate information is filled in to show negotiators a longitudinal pattern.

Example 5.1: Expense/Sales Ratio

Sales or income	Year 1	Year 2	Year 3
Cost of goods sold	This should be filled out to show a longitudinal pattern. The cost items on the left should be looked at as a percent of sales for each year.		
Gross profit			
Selling expense			
Operating profit			
Profit sharing			
Labor cost (where possible)			

There are other measures that are widely used in more general financial analysis, but these have less applicability to labor contract work. The degree of use is dependent on the industry and the financial structure of the companies within the industry. These include rate of return on company assets, which is calculated by dividing net income after taxes by total assets; net return on assets, found by dividing net income by sales and multiplying it times sales divided by assets; and rate of return on owners' investment, which is found by dividing net income after taxes by owners' investment. All three of these are calculated using information from the income statement, described in Exhibit 5.2. The above ratios concentrate on rate of return on monies invested by both company and owners. These ratios will come into use in discussions about an organization achieving an appropriate rate of return.

The management of the money position of the company may take many forms. Basically, most companies employ one or more of the following techniques:

1. Explore methods for the mobilization of money to reduce cash requirements;
2. Improve cash flow forecasting techniques, with the ultimate result of increasing reliability;
3. Pinpoint liquidity reserve needs;

4. Search continually for new and more productive uses of surplus money; and
5. Establish various sources of liquidity.

Implied thus far in the analysis of money management is the need to examine company operations with respect to expense outlay items. For labor negotiation teams, this provides strong arguments against claims of runaway cost of labor as the sole culprit in declining profits. Fixed assets are also involved in this analysis.

Fixed assets, as commonly described, have a limited life. In terms of flow of funds, depreciation of the fixed assets changes the amount of funds provided by operations. Depreciation permits keeping more monies after taxes and, as such, becomes an important aspect of money management.

The primary ratio for use in the analysis of fixed assets as a factor in management of monies deals with the turnover of net fixed assets in sales. This results in the index of efficiency and is calculated by dividing sales by net fixed assets. These figures are found on the balance sheet and income statement and are described in Exhibits 5.1 and 5.2. The index of efficiency presents a useful tool by which to judge whether fixed assets, such as plant, are being used to their maximum capacity. This figure must be interpreted with care. For example, utilities will have a low turnover of fixed assets, but have a high rate of profit on sales figure. Food stores will have a high rate of turnover of fixed assets, but a moderate to low rate of profit on sales.

To eliminate the problem of the amount of profit on sales in the ratio of sales to fixed assets, an alternative ratio may be used. The cost of goods manufactured, which is found on the income statement, may be used in lieu of sales to determine the relative use made of fixed assets in production sales. This figure, though not completely free of price variation and manufacturing distortions, will give a more precise measure than the prior one if such precision is required. It is calculated by dividing the cost of goods manufactured by net fixed assets.

RETURN ON INVESTMENT

The ratio of net profit after taxes to total assets yields a figure that reflects the value of capital to the company. It is calculated by dividing net profit after taxes by total assets, or by dividing net profits by sales and multiplying that times sales divided by assets. The balance sheet and income statement provide these figures (described in Exhibits 5.1 and 5.2). This form of analysis points out areas for improvement, such as where funds could be used better elsewhere in the company. Corporate managers recognize that capital is not available in unlimited quantitites and thus put a premium on its use. Up to this point, return-on-investment ratios were not used extensively by labor unions. It is not even given serious attention in Pillsbury's 1954 study. However, the current economic atmosphere and labor trends indicate it will become more important for both parties to use this type of analysis in preparation for negotiations.

Understanding areas for improvement is further aided by the advent of joint labor-management bargaining committees. The growing use of quality circles in the United States, labor representation on the Chrysler board of directors, and productivity bargaining elsewhere are positive signs that all parties are interested in and have something to gain from these improvements. Return on investment can be used by all parties throughout the company and its subsidiaries as a tool in gaining greater insight into these issues. It is a straightforward and easily understood tool.

In addition, two broad means for improving this ratio deserve attention: increasing the investment turnover and increasing the rate of profit on sales. Increasing the investment turnover is an area of investigation more readily accomplished by management through increased investment leverage and similar techniques. However, increasing the rate of profit on sales shows much promise for bipartisan action between labor and management groups. For the most part, this second means has been a one-sided affair in which management initiates action and labor remains somewhat suspicious of radical changes. This suspicion is often engendered by the fact that labor is not made an active partner in the process. Attempts to date reveal labor can contribute in a positive way to increasing this ratio. With added competitive pressure from foreign sources, labor should become active in this area. Labor involvement can be through joint committee efforts or quality circles. By these means, labor can offer help in areas of cost control that relate to the product as well as labor usage.

COMPARATIVE RATIO USE

Various ratios that are helpful to all parties have been discussed in the preceding sections. As mentioned previously, analysis of any ratio by itself for the current period may be difficult to interpret. It was suggested that financial data be kept for between five and ten years to allow for large individual ratio variations up or down. In addition, other standards for comparison can be used by both parties. Ratios can be compared to ratios of selected competing companies, same-industry ratios, and ratios of companies with the same union and similar composition of skills in the work force. Comparative ratio selection and where to find reliable information for comparison are the subjects of Chapter 7.

BREAK-EVEN ANALYSIS

In its most basic form, break-even analysis is an analytical tool for the study of the relationship between operating leverage and profits. For contract negotiations, it can be used to judge the impact of wage and benefit changes on company operations. Typically portrayed in chart form, it shows the point at which the company will make neither a profit nor a loss, specifically, the point at which sales are equal to costs.

Sales figures can be taken from the income statement. The gross margin most realistically reflects the company's ability to cover expenses. Total cost lines are computed by deducting net profits from sales or from other company financial reports. The total cost is then broken down into fixed and variable costs. Fixed charges usually include rent, interest, depreciation, plus general and administrative expenses. Note that although depreciation is a fixed cost, the amount varies depending on the method of depreciation and the estimated life expectancy. For example, the depreciation for the first year on a $1 million building can be as high as $120,000 or as low as $22,000. This is a big difference, but a "fixed" cost is controlled by management. Variable costs are derived by deducting fixed cost from total cost. The figure for sales is available from financial reports published by the company, as are the breakdowns that include labor cost. Labor cost should include as many of the fringe benefits that can be quantified in order to achieve maximum accuracy.

Exhibit 5.3 Break-even before Wage and Benefit Changes

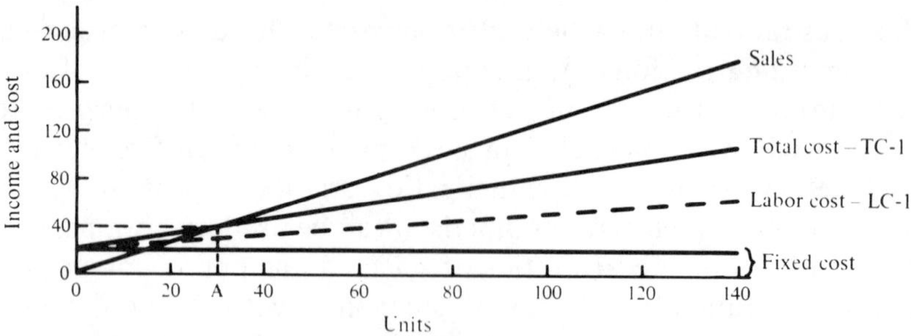

Exhibits 5.3 and 5.4 depict a hypothetical example of how changes in an area of variable cost may affect the break-even point by moving the required sales figure up if the cost moves up, assuming that all conditions remain the same. Note that this assumption is not always valid. Labor groups argue that increases in labor cost do not necessarily move in exact proportion to total cost, but that changes in quality and increased productivity may occur. Certain analysts in the field of finance and accounting suggest that changes in the price of labor should also prompt a review of the capital (machinery)-labor mix. This argument is covered in some detail in Chapter 6.

The illustrations used here suggest that a movement from point A to point B or from 30 to 75 units would be required to keep operations at a break-even point given the changes. Labor negotiators must

Exhibit 5.4 Break-even after Wage and Benefit Changes

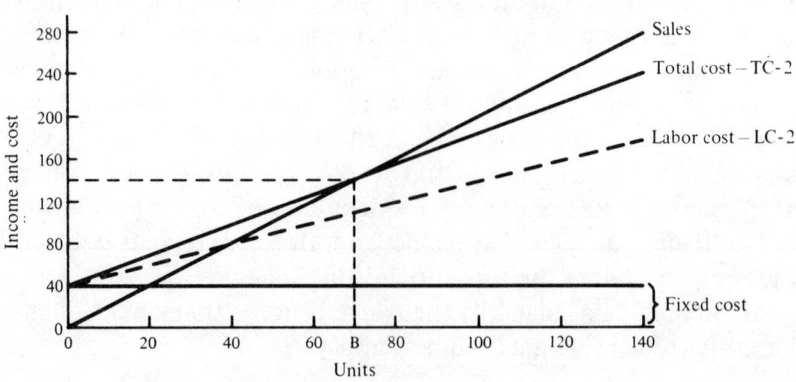

decide whether this is a representative picture. If not, they would then have to present arguments to refute the diagram. Note the movement of the increased labor cost (LC–1 and LC–2) and the total cost lines (TC-1 and TC-2) from chart to chart that resulted in the new break-even requirement at point B. The distance between the fixed cost lines and total cost lines are variable costs and include labor cost.

SUMMARY

Profits can be affected by relatively small changes of labor input. In an environment of strong international competition, the contract negotiator must have enough familiarity with the possible effects of any agreement on profitability.

The labor union negotiator is also fighting international competition. In this case, it is for domestic jobs. Jobs once held by domestic workers are now being handled by foreign workers. Skills in financial analysis can reveal if demands are truly too tough or if management's argument of moving to foreign soil because changes in labor costs are too harsh is inaccurate. If claims of management can be accurately and objectively examined from a financial perspective, perhaps solutions can be found in the process.

For both labor and management negotiators to produce more fruitful sessions, intelligent demands and counteroffers must be made. This involves the ability to be analytically objective as to the impact of the parties' actions on the company's overall financial status. The days of labor representatives presenting poorly devised or huge demands and hoping to "bargain out" with the biggest part are fast coming to an end. Company negotiators unskilled in the techniques required to fully assess the impact of demands are becoming rare. Attorneys versed only in labor law without training in how to figure the ramifications of contract proposals should no longer be considered skilled enough to be the prime component of a bargaining team. Increased productivity levels cannot be attained without active, rational, informed participation from all parties in the negotiation process. This involves possession of the skills necessary to make and analyze reasonable and intelligent demands.

6

The Effect of Contract Proposals on Other Operations of the Company

INTRODUCTION

Personnel involved in the labor relations process must be aware of the effect of contract proposals on other operations of the company. Steel industry negotiations, for example, resulted in the need for millions of added sales to cover the cost of only a fraction of a cent increase for wages and benefits. Arguments of "management slack" and other areas of corporate inefficiency aside, contract proposals have far-reaching effects on company operations. Managerial slack refers to institutional inefficiencies in the corporate organization that demonstrate that profit maximization is not necessarily a prime goal of managers. Herbert Simon, one of the chief developers of this idea, believes there are numerous examples of managers spending corporate profits on their own (not illegal) goals, such as posh executive offices and expensive automobiles.

While union negotiators request items that are for the benefit of their members, and while they may calculate some specific costs differently from management, they do not disclaim the direct impact of proposals. It is therefore, clearly, an important function for both union and company negotiators to assume responsibility for assessing the consequences of demands. It is a particularly important function of management to figure when and how the union request will affect the various parts of the company's operations. To judge the impact on cost-price-volume and other relationships accurately, certain techniques and skills must be understood. These involve being able to figure the various relationships among cost, price, and volume and the contributions each area makes to company operations.

THE CONCEPT OF CONTRIBUTION MARGINS

A fundamental way to look at the relationships among changes in labor cost, price, and volume is the concept of the contribution to overhead and to profit. In its most basic form, contribution can be defined as the difference between the price of a product and average variable cost. The concept of contribution is a powerful analytical tool used primarily to judge the effects of product, price, and volume changes on company profit levels. It is not a highly refined method, but it is quick and handy. With minor adjustments, it can be useful to labor contract analysts to judge how a request for a wage increase, for example, will affect the amount of funds remaining for profit distribution.

The theory behind the idea of contribution, often referred to as the contribution margin, is that money received from the sale of a product covers first the costs of making and selling the product and then fixed or capacity-creating costs. Whatever remains is reinvested, paid out in taxes, distributed as profits, or some combination of the three. To illustrate the concept of contribution, the following example is used:

Example 6.1:

Net sales (100,000 units @ $7.50)		$750,000
Cost of goods sold		
Direct labor	150,000	
Materials	112,500	
Supervision, payroll taxes, etc.	187,500	
		450,000
Gross profit		300,000
Selling and administrative expense		150,000
Profit before taxes		150,000

$$\text{Profit per unit} \quad \frac{\$150{,}000 \text{ profit}}{100{,}000 \text{ units}} = \$1.50/\text{unit}$$

Average variable cost		
Materials		$112,000
Labor		150,000
Commission (10% selling price)		75,000
Total average variable cost		$337,000

$$\text{Variable cost per unit} \quad \frac{\$337{,}000}{100{,}000 \text{ units}} = \$3.37/\text{unit}$$

Contribution	
Selling price/unit	$7.50
Average variable cost/unit	3.37
Total contribution/unit	$4.13

In the above case, $4.13 per unit is available for use in meeting fixed costs. The amount that remains when fixed costs are deducted represents money that can be reinvested, paid out in taxes, or distributed as profits.

Break-even points were discussed earlier as a means of assessing the impact of changes in labor cost. Break-even analysis can also arrive at more precise volume and price figures that can be used in judging changes in variable costs such as labor.

First, it is necessary to understand the general break-even point formula, which is:

$$\text{Break-even point} = \frac{\text{Fixed costs}}{\text{Contribution per unit}}$$

Using the figures from Example 6.1, fixed cost would be $262,500 (supervision, payroll taxes, and so forth $187,500 + $75,000 from selling and administrative expenses), which divided by the contribution figure of $4.13 per unit would equal a break-even volume of 63,559 units.

$$\text{Break-even volume} = \frac{\$262{,}500}{\$4.13} = 63{,}559 \text{ units}$$

This volume level is somewhat below the 100,000 unit projected sales volume. Remember, the same criticisms noted on break-even analysis earlier still apply. The above figure is still a result of estimates and judgments regarding cost divisions between fixed and variable. But for the purposes of evaluation for contract negotiation, that figure will lend itself to the type of approximation necessary to support or refute demands.

The impact of a 10 percent increase in the labor cost factor (variable cost) as a result of a union demand must also be considered. This, of course, would be figured in similar fashion by both sides at the bargaining table using cost-volume analysis. In this case, the contribution per unit will be decreased by \$.15 per unit (.10 X \$150,000 = \$15,000 - 100,000 = .15)

$$\text{Break-even volume} = \frac{\$262{,}500}{3.98} = 65{,}955 \text{ units}$$

This will require an increase of 2,396 units in volume over the prior level break-even volume.

Example 6.2: The effect on profits resulting from this demand:

Net sales		\$750,000
Cost goods sold		
Direct labor	165,000	
Materials	112,500	
Supervisor, taxes	187,500	
		465,000
Gross profit		\$285,000
Selling and administrative expenses		150,000
Profit before taxes		\$135,000

OR

Selling price	\$7.50
Average variable cost	3.52
Contribution to fixed costs and profits	\$3.98
Fixed cost per unit	2.63
Profit per unit	\$1.35

100,000 units X \$1.35/unit = \$135,000 profit.

The prior profit level was \$1.50 per unit. The change in labor cost has reduced this to \$1.35 or a 15¢ loss in revenue per unit (see Example 6.2). Despite the wishes of the board of directors, this could affect the price-earnings ratio of a company and its stock's selling price, especially if competitive conditions rule out a price increase.

COST-PRICE ANALYSIS

Cost-price analysis can be used to determine the level to which product prices might have to be raised in order to maintain profit margins and the impact those price changes might have. This type of analysis becomes important in addressing the fact that managers of companies have an implied responsibility to their investors—in spite of the implicit risk involved in any investment—to make every attempt to offer a return for the use of their funds.

Consider the example of a company that wishes to maintain a 20 percent profit margin before taxes as protection from the effects of inflation. The price formula used for a specified profit margin taken from Christenson, Vancil, and Marshall (1973) indicates that the price per unit can be found by dividing total fixed cost by the company's estimated sales volume and adding the variable costs per unit. This figure is then divided by the net revenue percentage, which is found by dividing 100 percent into 100 percent minus the profit margin the company wishes to maintain. Example 6.3, which uses the same figures, indicates that the price that would have to be charged is \$7.69.

Example 6.3:

$$\text{Price/unit} = \left(\frac{\text{Total fixed cost}}{\text{Estimated volume}} + \frac{\text{Variable cost}}{\text{Unit}}\right) \div \frac{\text{Net revenue}}{100\%}$$

$$\text{Price/unit} = \left(\frac{262{,}500}{100{,}000} + 3.52\right) \div \frac{80\%}{100\%}$$

$$= (2.63 + 3.52) \div .8$$

$$= 6.15 \div .8$$

$$= \$7.69$$

An important assumption that must be made in this type of calculation is the estimated sales volume. The usefulness of this assumption is contingent on whether the company can sell this volume at the calculated price. Earlier calculations indicate that when the contribution margin is reduced the volume requirement becomes 65,955 units, which is below the 100,000 projected sales volume. In this case, the most important consideration would be whether the product is highly price sensitive in a competitive market to a 19¢ price increase. (Its previous price was $7.50.)

Labor negotiators argue that gains in the efficiency of operations will offset labor cost increases so that a reasonable profit can be achieved without price increases. This was a sound argument prior to 1973, when the nation's output per hour was rising at sufficient levels to allow for improvements in wage and benefit items with only modest price changes. Since 1973 these claims are more difficult to support. The growth in productivity in terms of output per hour has been disappointing. Reasons offered range from lack of investment in research and development to changing attitudes of workers. For purposes of analysis regarding financial implications of labor relations decisions, the cause of the decline is not very important. What is important are changes in product mix and price, and the changes in sales volume as a result of changes in labor cost. The argument of increased efficiency offsetting cost increases does not apply uniformly. As such, it becomes important for negotiators to estimate the effect of contract changes on profit, price, and break-even volume. They must also consider whether sales projections are realistic, the level of product price sensitivity, and other similar benchmarks.

This type of analysis creates an armory of valuable evidence for use by both sides at the bargaining table. Given the reasonable availability of information, union negotiators can use the same techniques as management negotiators to develop sound, logical demands and defend their positions with regard to potential impact on the organization.

EFFECT ON NONUNION WORKERS

Parties to the negotiation process must also be aware of the impact of the results of negotiations on other workers. According to one survey of contract-costing practices, few companies make a detailed estimate of package impact on other workers (Granof 1973). Furthermore, only a minority show more than cursory recognition of the fact that the agreed-to changes will have an effect on other workers.

Most firms automatically grant nonunion employees all increases in wages and benefits negotiated for union employees. As implied in previous sections, negotiators should cost proposals considering the total work force. This gives a detailed estimate of spillover effect and can be added to the add-on cost figures to give a package effect.

Data requirements and procedures for costing changes are the same for nonunion employees as for employees covered in the collective bargaining agreement.

IMPACT ON PROFITS USING ONLY TRADITIONAL COSTING METHODS

A number of points should be considered when estimating the impact of negotiations on profits or budgets. One major area is the weakness of the four commonly accepted costing techniques: total annual cost, cost per employee per year, percent of payroll, and cost per hour. These were discussed at some length in Chapter 2 and have been used in examples throughout the book.

The principal drawback of the generally used methods is that they lack meaningful correlation to decisions that have to be made at the corporate level. While they do provide general guidance, this is often considered misleading guidance. For instance, certain clauses that do not appear to be directly relevant to compensation (such as work schedules, job classifications, and seniority) are not easily quantifiable; yet, they may have significant financial impact.

Consider also how elusive the important relationships between a company's labor cost and other aspects of its operations can be. Changes in volume, product mix, and capital investment are very likely to influence the amount of labor used by the company. Conversely, any changes in the amount of labor needed or its cost will affect volume, product mix, and capital investment needs.

As explained by writers in the field, there is not always a clear-cut relationship between increasing labor cost and the price of a product. That is, there is no definite indication than an increase in wages will result in an increase in product costs and a subsequent increase in price.

The weakness of the four commonly accepted expressions for costing labor contracts results from four prime oversights. First of all, they fail to clarify how companies will adjust to new labor contracts. Second, they generally fail to include opportunity cost. Third, both cash flow and time value of money are not represented. Fourth, they fail to consider the costs and relative values of alternatives such as other employment sources.

How companies will adapt to changes in the labor contract should be viewed from a planning perspective. Changes in labor cost should prompt a total review of price, product mix, and other factors that go into making the product.

If the company has several products, it is unlikely the ratio of labor cost to total cost will be identical for all products. When wages are increased, more labor-intensive products may become less profitable relative to the other goods produced. This leads companies to decrease production of labor-intensive items and increase production of others. If the company reacts to increased wages with a corresponding price increase and customers fail to accept it, revenues will decline.

Raising prices as a reflex action can be avoided. If the firm is operating with the optimum proportion of labor to machinery, a wage increase should prompt a review of this relationship. Increased labor costs may make use of a higher proportion of machinery to labor more economically feasible. In this case, the company may not have to increase its product price and, since less labor will be required, an unnecessary impasse over a wage increase can be avoided at the bargaining table. The above is in contrast to the traditional approach of simply multiplying hours worked by the proposed wage increase.

Referring to the information in Example 6.1, the cost of a 10 percent increase in wages can result in either a decrease in profit contribution per unit of 15¢ ($1.50/unit minus $1.35/unit) or an increase in the product price of 19¢ per unit. Management may feel either alternative to be detrimental, which could result in an impasse over this item. Yet, certain adjustments in the production process may make the higher wage rate feasible. Technological changes may allow for the raise to be granted and result in sufficient savings so as not to necessitate raising the price.

For example, technical adjustments could now be made that result in the fixed cost increasing by 25¢ per unit while labor, with a wage increase of 10 percent, shows a net decrease of 15¢ per unit, and materials cost decreases by 10¢ per unit (such as reduced scrap waste).

Example 6.4:

	Revised contribution		Prior contribution	
Income per unit		$7.50		$7.50
Variable cost				
Materials	$1.02		$1.12	
Labor	1.35		1.50	
Commissions	.75	3.02	.75	3.37
Contribution to fixed cost and profit		$4.38		$4.13
Fixed cost		2.88		2.63
Contribution to profit		$1.50		$1.50

$1.50 per unit X 100,000 units = $150,000 profit before taxes.

In Example 6.4 the position of the company is unaffected by the wage demand; the company will not have to raise its price nor will there be an unnecessary impasse over a wage increase. This example illustrates that bargaining can become a more sophisticated process when certain factors are considered.

Of course, one must consider the possible resulting layoffs. These would not be desirable from the point of view of either party, but neither is a strike desirable. If the number of people involved is small, arrangements, such as using attrition in lieu of mass layoffs, could be made. This could reduce the immediate effect of the savings, but might be well worth the investment. Such a tactic can establish trust and good faith and set of precedent for future technological change.

Failure to consider opportunity costs is the second problem with traditional costing techniques. Opportunity cost is the cost of choosing one course of action over another. That is, by the definition offered by economists, opportunity cost is the return on investment that would have been received if the resource (in this case, labor input) would have been used in the best alternative opportunity. For example, if there is a demand by the union to increase the lunch period from 30 to 60 minutes, management traditionally looks at whether the company wishes to spend this money on lunch periods or a best next alternative investment. The traditional decision point is the opportunity cost of the money that would be invested in lunch versus machinery or whatever use might have been elected.

There is another level on which one can view opportunity cost in the lunchtime extension demand. If the workers are on the job the same number of hours but work time is reduced 30 minutes because of the increased lunch benefit, then less product is being made. Now, the opportunity cost becomes the loss of revenue from finished products. It becomes more critical if the plant is operating three shifts at capacity, which would mean overtime could not be used to make up for the lost 30 minutes of production per shift.

The cost of the added time for the lunch break may be viewed in terms of the lost revenue from product sales. The opportunity cost decision at this point is the utilization of 30 minutes of labor input per shift.

The third area of concern with regard to traditional costing techniques centers on cash flow and the time value of money. Most contracts (77 percent) extend for a three-year period (BNA 1983). The cost to the firm of borrowed funds or capital is generally greater than 10 percent, making the time value of money a significant item in calculating labor cost. A benefit granted in the third year of a contract is less costly than an equal benefit offered in the first year.

These facts imply a need to consider the financial theory of capital budgeting when costing labor contracts. The concept offers genuine potential for analysis of comparative contract proposals. As the bargaining process becomes more sophisticated and computer-programming models gain wider usage, capital budgeting will increase. When the entire labor package is balanced against other costs and income sources, individuals with backgrounds in economics will see theory applications, with minor adjustments, resembling general equilibrium models.

In its basic form, capital budgeting is an application of classic economic theory. A company should operate where its marginal revenue is equal to its marginal cost (Ferguson and Gould 1975). When extended to the capital-budgeting process, marginal cost is the company's percentage cost of capital (Brigham and Pappas 1972). Marginal revenue is the addition to total revenue that results from the sale of one more unit of output and represents a rate of change in total revenue. Building on this definition, marginal cost is the extra cost of producing one more unit of output. These costs can be easily noted by the change in total cost of that unit.

Table 6.1 Present Value of $1 at Compound Interest (percent)

Periods hence	7	8	10	12	14	15
1	0.935	0.926	0.909	0.893	0.877	0.870
2	0.873	0.857	0.826	0.797	0.796	0.756
3	0.816	0.794	0.751	0.712	0.675	0.658
4	0.763	0.735	0.683	0.636	0.592	0.572
5	0.713	0.681	0.621	0.567	0.519	0.497
6	0.666	0.630	0.565	0.507	0.456	0.432
7	0.623	0.584	0.513	0.452	0.400	0.376
8	0.582	0.540	0.513	0.452	0.400	0.376
9	0.544	0.500	0.424	0.361	0.308	0.284
10	0.508	0.463	0.386	0.322	0.270	0.247
15	0.362	0.315	0.239	0.183	0.140	0.123
20	0.258	0.215	0.149	0.104	0.073	0.061

In labor negotiations, the process becomes one of measurement of costs associated with particular union demands extended into the future. Following this difficult assessment, the costs are discounted back over the life of the "investment" (demand) using the internal rate of return (often called hurdle rate) of the company as the percentage factor. An internal rate of return is a percentage figure that the company feels is necessary to achieve on its invested funds. In some cases the internal rate of return is the cost to the company of borrowed money (capital). Alternative solutions to labor demands can then be ranked using present value tables or the standard formula.

The standard formula is: $PV = V/(1 - i)^N$ where PV is the present value, V is the equivalent future value in N periods to come, i is the discount rate or company cost of capital figure, and N is the number of years of expected length of the flow. Tables exist that can be used to find present values at various interest rates when calculating. An example is found in Table 6.1. Present value tables tell how much money must be set aside today to have a certain amount in the future, or how much a future amount of money would be worth if it could be had today. For example, assume the cost of capital is 12 percent and one is looking at a five-year time horizon—what will the current value of a $100 return be in five years? Look at Table 6.1, go down the left column marked periods hence to five, read over to the 12 percent column, and record the figure 0.567. Multiply this figure by $100 and the present value of the return is $56.70. Calculating the present value of future money flows is often referred to as "discounting."

Costs associated with particular demands may be difficult to pinpoint because they vary with respect to how far into the future they extend. Do they extend for the life of the current contract or several successive contracts? Does the analysis use the same long-term planning horizons as the company? Is the offer to be "front-end loaded" (is the increase granted immediately) or spread over the contract period? Costs in each of these cases could have the same present value during the current contract period, but could vary significantly if extended to several contracts.

The concept of discounting has potential in figuring alternative offers and requests in the bargaining process. For example, when management makes its best offer or labor makes a request and it is not accepted by the other party, an impasse may be avoided by figuring other combinations in discounted form that result in the same net percent value as what was rejected. If one of these alternative forms is acceptable, a strike may be averted.

Consider an example of a company negotiating a two-year contract. The internal rate of return or company cost of capital is 15 percent. The offer by management is for 75¢ for each year of the contract—frontloaded. This is based on an assumed average wage rate of $5.00 per hour. The union has rejected this offer, wanting more, but is willing to accept it spread over a two-year period. Example 6.5 uses the figures in Table 6.1 to calculate the present value of management's offer.

Example 6.5:

Initial management offer
(using present value table in the 15% column)

First year	(5.00 + .75 increase) × .870	= $5.002
Second year	(5.00 + .75 increase) × .756	= 4.347
Total present value of the management offer		= $9.349

The present value computations for the initial management offer yield a value to the company of $9.349. The goal of the negotiating team is to find an alternative the union will accept, yet with the same present value.

To compute the alternative package, total present value of the wages of the contract must equal $9.349, the amount management is able to afford. To find alternatives acceptable to the parties, the following format is used: ($5.00 + I).870 + ($5.00 + 2I).756 = $9.349. If I stands for the increase the first year and 2I the second-year increase, the present value figures from the table are used in the formula to solve for I, the increase amount. When solved, I equals .512 and the alternative package may be computed that will have the same present value as the prior offer, but may satisfy the union demand for a larger increase. The wage offers become $.512 or $5.12 ($5.00 + .512) for the first year and $1.024 or $6.024 ($6.00 + 2(.512)) for the second year (see Example 6.6). Note that this is only one of many possible combinations that could be worked out. Note also that most unions would prefer the reverse of this hypothesized solution and want more money up front in the first year of the contract. If that is the case, alternatives can be developed using that as the variable factor. Also, keep in mind that, as explained in Chapter 2, if an increase is broken up so as to be granted on a quarterly basis, the cost will decrease.

Example 6.6:

Alternative management offer

First year	$5.512 X .870	=	$4.795
Second year	$6.024 X .756	=	4.554
Total present value of alternative offer		=	$9.349

The alternative package to the union ($.512 + $.1024 = $1.536) results in an added 3.6 or 4¢ above the first offer ($.75 + .75 = $1.50) that was rejected, but has the same present value cost to management. As pointed out earlier, the company must decide if it wishes to have an ending contract period wage of $6.54 ($5.00 + 1.536 = $6.536 or 6.54) per hour versus $6.50 ($5.00 + $1.50 = $6.50). The 4¢ difference does obviously influence future contract negotiations since this will be the new starting point.

When the time value of money is a factor in management decision-making, discounting or present value calculations can provide a framework for making negotiation decisions that uses the same language used in decision-making in other areas of the company (such as for decisions on equipment or new business ventures).

Costing Alternative Employment Sources

The above discussion of developing alternatives based on equal present value of flows to satisfy union requests may be more complex than it originally appears. Specifically, if employee investment decisions can be written in the same language as any other investment, then the company can compare it with alternative work force options. One such theme growing in popularity is the use of robots.

The formula for figuring the investment worth for robots, as for other capital investments, includes figuring how long it take to recoup the cost of the initial investment, often called the payback period. The payback period is the initial investment divided by the average savings in production costs over the useful life of the robot. Some industry reports show a payback period for robots of less than two years (Lundquist 1982).

Iron Age ("Welding and Robotics") cites an example of calculation that would identify the payback period for a robot used for welding (see Example 6.7). Costs of employees to operate should also be included when applicable.

Example 6.7:

$$\text{Payback} = \frac{I}{DW + DA + RS + DT - M - O +/- q\,(DW + Z)}$$

I = initial investment
DW = displaced workers' salaries
DA = zero minus average annual displaced automation machinery costs
RS = estimate for average annual savings from using the robot
D = robot depreciation
t = .5 minus the tax rate
O = operating cost of robot equipment
q = 20 percent minus production rate coefficient
z = capital value of equipment

It is not the point of this volume to debate the merits of robotics, but rather to show that future decisions about alternatives can be part of the analysis of labor contract costs. This capability brings the negotiation process closer to a model of rational economic decision-making.

Possible Solutions to Traditional Costing Method Problems

What can be done to help correct the problems identified with traditional costing methods? To begin with, awareness of their shortcomings and a careful consideration of the relationships among labor cost, volume, product mix, and capital investment will help. As most business executives know, understanding the problem is the first step to finding solutions. In this case, awareness will help companies adapt to the new labor contract.

Awareness is important when referring to opportunity cost, but further investigation may also be necessary. For such areas as cash flow and time value of money, it may be helpful to apply techniques commonly used in evaluating all long-range capital investments.

The discounted cash-flow model, which defines the incremental cash flows that result from accepting a project, is particularly useful. To construct these models, use internal rate of return (hurdle rate) as the percentage, discount the cash flow back over the life of the project, and rank the alternatives according to magnitude of net cash flow. This added step in preparation is to allow for a better comparison among alternative proposals since they would be in common terms (present value dollar terms). Other advantages include requiring the company to estimate exact cash flows involved in each contract clause proposal. This will consider more than direct cost as calculated by conventional methods and forces consideration of added effects on other aspects of company operations, such as price, volume, and product mix.

Granof reveals that few companies utilize discounted cash-flow models, although some companies do study the important cash flows associated with contract changes and also base labor cost projections on estimated planning volume. This added step in costing union proposals requires only minor extensions of current practices.

Data requirements of this technique are such that no special information is required. Discounting is useful because it enables both management and labor to formulate wage packages that are affordable and to determine other patterns of increases that will have the same discounted cost. The matter becomes a function of substitution into the appropriate discounting formula.

Note that there are various conditions or situations that would make the discounted values objectionable to management (such as higher ending wage levels) and that the method does not make conventional techniques obsolete. It is intended to be an added step or a way to prompt awareness of overall company operations and to avoid serious miscalculations at the bargaining table that have come from not investigating contract proposals in adequate depth.

SUMMARY

Chapter 6 takes the reader into a discussion of how the contract agreement can affect the many other operations of a company. Much of the subject matter is not considered conventional material in the labor relations area. Yet as the chapter discusses, these subjects are taking on increased importance due to their impact on company profitability.

The chapter begins with a discussion of contribution to overhead and profit of the company. Examples are offered regarding how an increased wage demand can alter the amount of contribution remaining for profit distribution. The concept of contribution margins is then merged with break-even analysis (discussed graphically in Chapter 5) to assess the impact of wage changes on required sales volume to support the new wage level. Sales volume and selling price are often topics discussed together. This chapter merges these topics with the idea of profit margins—that is, to what level will prices need to be raised in order to maintain company profit margins?

The impact of contract changes is not limited to the above items. The chapter discusses the impact of negotiated changes on workers not covered by the collective bargaining agreement, an item that often receives little recognition from companies.

The chapter then compares the impact on profits using the basic costing techniques in Chapter 2 and Chapter 6. While helpful and necessary, the techniques in Chapter 2 (total annual cost, cost per employee per year, percent of payroll, and cost per hour) result in several oversights. They fail to show how companies will adjust to the new contract, fail to include opportunity cost, do not take into account time value of money, and fail to consider alternative employment sources.

The chapter offers solutions in the form of discounting of wage offers and setting contribution margins that will support technical change in order to decrease overall labor cost and evaluate alternative employment sources. Solutions are discussed in terms of individual tools for the labor contract analyst and as an integrated approach to pull together the labor negotiation and other operations of the company.

7

Disclosure Requirements, Information Sources, and Comparative Data

INTRODUCTION

Locating pertinent information can be difficult when investigating projected proposal costs. Problems that are encountered range from how much information must be supplied to make a reasonable assessment to what specific information is applicable and in what form it is to be presented.

This chapter is designed to aid in those investigations by providing a broader pool of sources from which to draw the data necessary for a thorough assessment. Previous chapters have contained references to techniques available for cost analysis. References to works that expand on the topics discussed in each chapter can be found by chapter in Appendix C. This chapter will provide additional sources of information for use in comparative analysis, such as information in the financial rates analysis area and information regarding legal requirements pertaining to disclosure of information. Information is also included on a variety of other topics that might be of interest to the investigator, such as information about local, industry, and national wage rates for specific job categories and how individual financial ratios compare with those of similar companies in the same industry.

DISCLOSURE REQUIREMENTS

In the case of *NLRB* v. *Truit Manufacturing Company*, a significant point relevant to the legal limits of the supplying of comparative data was settled (351 US 149). It was ruled that any relevant information necessary for knowledgeable consideration of the employer's position under the auspices of union representation must be provided when requested. A broad range of data falls under this ruling. Items within these guidelines include job description and classification data, time and motion study information, wage information, and the right to conduct independent surveys regarding policy. Of greater significance to the purposes examined here, the ruling upheld the right of negotiators to request financial information to support employer claims of inability to meet union requests and comparative wage data to support claims of noncompetitive rates (Twomey 1980). A noncooperative attitude with regard to requests in these areas may result in a finding of bad-faith bargaining.

Although these rulings have done much to aid the gathering of comparative data, there have been no legal stipulations regarding what form this information must take. Consequently, the management negotiating team is not required to prepare orderly answers in the form requested by the union team.

This section will offer some guidance as to available research sources. It also suggests a starting point for those unfamiliar with the information-gathering process and may help negotiators to ask the correct questions and make intelligent, responsible, and realistic demands.

DATA SOURCES FOR LABOR NEGOTIATORS

Unions generally do not have immediate access to company records. Management and legal thought behind this policy lies in the feeling that open access would harm the competitive nature of the company and be a relinquishment of managerial rights; whether this feeling is true is the subject of much debate. There are certain areas in which companies have been required to furnish information to investigators (Anderson 1975). These are outlined below and include reference sources where more information may be obtained, along with any recent changes.

1. Information about the cost of proposed improvements to welfare programs, pension, and insurance data: 61 LRRM 2657, 32 LRMM 2225.

LRRM refers to *Labor Relations Reference Manual*, published by the Bureau of National Affairs, Inc. The LRRM covers decisions of the courts and the National Labor Relations Board (NLRB). The manual consists of three sections. The first includes abbreviations, parallel table of NLRB decisions, table of cases, and parallel citations for court cases. The second section contains summaries of all published NLRB decisions. The third section contains the full text of U.S. Supreme Court, U.S. Courts of Appeals, and other federal and state court decisions. There is a complete explanation of how to use the LRRM in the front section of that work.

2. Wage and benefit data for grouping of people outside the bargaining unit: 81 LRRM 1420.

3. Accurate dollar figures paid to workers, including what is agreed to above contract figures: 69 LRRM 1100.

4. Dates of hire and seniority position of workers: 36 LRRM 2576.

5. Number of hours worked by every worker: 34 LRRM 1319.

6. Pay rates and spreads for job classifications and descriptions: 32 LRRM 2709.

7. Criteria for pay raises: 26 LRRM 1333.

8. Factory productivity changes: 30 LRRM 1265. (Anderson 1975).

Stockholders who are union members have no guarantee of greater access to company records. Stockholders' rights are limited to receiving only information regarding the financial health of the company. A direct approach members might choose to gain the desired information would be to negotiate a clause giving access to financial records and tax returns. However, the frequency of such a policy change is rare and, despite the increase of union representation on the board of directors, disclosure of additional information does not seem forthcoming in the near future.

Another item of concern to unions is the desire for an adjustment in policies regarding disclosure of information from closely held corporations, that is, those companies where stock is controlled by a family or a few individuals. There are a number of methods employed by unions to monitor the productivity of and gain financial information for contract preparation from such companies. One method is to keep track of shipments of incoming materials. Overhead cost figures can be estimated by applying the appropriate industry figures or ratios. While certainly not precise, this estimate forms a base upon which further estimates may be made.

These initial estimates can be made more accurate by drawing upon discussions between union officials and people in the industry with the appropriate knowledge to fill in data gaps. Officers of competing companies, suppliers, equipment manufacturers, and others often have a great amount of information regarding the financial affairs of their industry. In addition, there are various federal and state sources of information as well as reporting services that can be utilized. The result is the development of a general body of knowledge giving union negotiators a better balance of information on which to construct intelligent demands.

As in the case of companies that must because of legal reasons supply data to unions, federal and state sources do not tend to supply information in readily usable form to unions. This does not come from a desire to be difficult, but rather because the reporting requirements of data are not necessarily in a form designed to augment labor relations or any other specific area of concern. For example, the principal intention of reports filed by companies to the Securities and Exchange Commission is not contract analysis. Yet, certain information regarding salary, bonus, stock options, and other vital data can be extracted from these reports. The most useful data included by these companies are contained in the prospectus reports of new stock or bond offerings, which cover current data on debt structures, officer compensation, and proposed use of new funds.

Companies file a great deal of paperwork with regulatory commissions. Unions and other interested parties have access to most of these mountains of paperwork. Regulatory groups receiving information include the Interstate Commerce Commission, the Federal Power Commission, the Civil Aeronautics Board, the Federal Communications Commission, and the Federal Trade Commission. Reports are also published by the Treasury Department, the Department of Housing and Urban Development, the Department of Labor, the Department of Commerce, and Bureau of the Census. The Department of Housing and Urban Development in Washington, D.C., for example, maintains files on land developers, including information on property descriptions and financial data. These are available for a modest copying fee.

The type and number of reports vary among agencies depending on budget levels. The most accurate method of choosing publications for a specific contract investigation is to write for a publications list from the Government Printing Office in Washington, D.C.

Some union organizations have sophisticated research departments with accurate records to facilitate gathering data for bargaining. Files include past data and information for future use. Public sector unions are aided in their searches by the Freedom of Information Act allowing access to data necessary for bargaining. Still other unions are in a cooperative bargaining scenario in which information is shared between the parties in the cooperative. After a number of contract negotiations have occurred, most bargaining units have a relatively accurate accumulation of information on which to base estimated revisions for any proposed demands.

State governments and agencies are sometimes able to provide information where federal sources cannot. For example, companies are not required to file information with the Securities and Exchange Commission if the number of shareholders is below a certain number. However, states do require that a complete financial report be filed, and this information is generally available from the office of the Secretary of State where the company headquarters are located.

DATA SOURCES FOR COMPANY NEGOTIATORS

As indicated earlier, companies are required to furnish union bargaining teams with information sufficient to formulate intelligent demands. There are, however, certain limits to the degree of cooperation and burden-to-suffer to provide requested information (Anderson 1975). Below are listed some of the various constraints on data sharing between corporations and union bargaining teams.

1. The cost of gathering requested information by the union may have to be borne by them: 35 LRRM 2730.

2. Where information is very hard to locate, as in detailed combinations of past earnings of workers, the company may decline the union demand: 47 LRRM 1072.

3. The company may require the union to examine the information on their premises for job-evaluation records, job-description records, and customer and supplier information: 47 LRRM 1039, 47 LRRM 1472; and an audit of relevant records by a licensed or certified public accountant chosen by the union: 47 LRRM 1472.

4. Technical information on how the job analysis was put together, for example, the point system used, does not have to be given to the union: 57 LRRM 1001.

5. Cost data on noncontributory items, such as group dental coverage, do not have to be furnished: 48 LRRM 2313 (Anderson 1975).

While the above is not an exhaustive list, it does demonstrate that information need not be freely given the union bargaining team. Currently, there is a growing body of practitioners and academicians that believes the more open both sides can be in the data-gathering process, the better the bargaining outcome will be. An open attitude of mutual good faith tends to foster a problem-solving atmosphere and provides more workable contract proposals.

A company's own internal data sources are assumed to be accessible for comparative studies; however, no claims can be made as to the easy acquisition of such information. Previously in this book, a great deal of time has been devoted to discussing the pursuit of data and the form it may take. Further discussion will offer sources that will provide effective comparisons to substantiate claims made at the bargaining table regarding accepted practices and what pertinent information is being offered by the companies or industries being investigated.

Various categories of information may be of interest to the contract analyst. Categories selected to describe information sources, which closely follow those subject areas catalogued by most libraries, include: industrial overview, individual company, historical, biographical, current financial, past financial, comparative financial, and statistical. These eight categories are sufficiently narrow to allow researchers to pinpoint where to find the type of data they require. Most college or university libraries have information available on all of these topics and subscribe to many of the publications listed in Table 7.1. This table contains areas of overlap in some topics in the event certain public libraries do not subscribe to some of the listed references. Individual company or organization reference sources are another area of information.

Bureau of Labor statistics and other data compiled by government sources are more specific and comprehensive than those listed in Table 7.1. The information contained in these bureau files is complex enough to justify their own reference listings. Availability of subject compilations depend, for a particular geographic location, on whether the local library facility is a Federal Documents depository and whether the particular depository subscribes to a specific area of research. Some libraries carry only a limited number of items in print, with additional items on microfilm or some similar system.

If a local library is a Federal Documents depository, its librarian will have a master list of published government documents. Searching this reference is the quickest way to find items of interest. Librarians can be of great assistance in the area of searching government documents, which can be very complex.

Subscription services are also good sources of information for contract analysts. Areas these services cover include statistical, legal, and general labor relations questions. None of these services offers direct guidance in computing the cost of a labor contract or its implications for other company operations.

Three principal subscription services often found in company/organization in-house files or local college libraries are Commerce Clearing House, Prentice-Hall, and the Bureau of National Affairs. All are private corporations and maintain sales and service staffs to aid subscribing organizations in utilizing their services. Following are some topics of special interest to contract analysts on which these services can provide detailed information as defined by each service company.

Commerce Clearing House provides:

1. *Labor Law Guide*, which supplies quick answers to everyday questions arising under federal and state requirements that regulate the employer-employee relationship. It covers federal and state laws governing labor relations, including wages and hours laws, fair employment practices, union contracts, cost-of-living index, labor and management reporting disclosures, internal union affairs, and federal controls.

2. *Human Resources Management*, which supplies fingertip access to a wide range of compensation problems faced by personnel professionals. The volume includes a review of federal and state minimum wage, overtime pay, and the full text of federal wage law and key regulations.

3. *Employment Relations*, which supplies access to employment relations problems. The volume contains explanation of federal and state labor relations laws. Specific areas include problems of the nonunion employer, union campaigns, elections, contract clauses, grievances and arbitration, and strikes and enforcement.

4. *Human Resources Management: Ideas and Trends in Personnel*, which focuses on trends in compensation, employment relations, EEO/Affirmative Action, and personnel practices and communications.

5. *Personnel Guide*, which covers such topics as hiring, firing, seniority rights, discrimination, safety, employee's rights, and management rights.

Table 7.1 Reference Sources

Statistical and financial sources	Industrial/organization overview	Individual company/organization	Historical	Biographical	Current financial	Past financial	Projected financial	Comparative financial
U.S. Industrial Outlook	X		X				X	
Standard & Poor's Industry	X	X	X					
Predicasts Basebook	X					X		X
Predict's Annual Cumulative Edition	X					X		X
The Value Line: Part I Summary and Index	X	X			X	X	X	X
Troy's Almanac of Business & Industrial Financial Ratios	X						X	
Standard & Poor's Standard Corporation Descriptions Index Section in 7 Volumes	X	X	X	X	X	X	X	X
Moody's								
Industrial	X	X	X	X	X	X	X	X
Over-the-Counter	X	X	X	X	X	X	X	X
Transportation	X	X	X	X	X	X	X	X
Bank and Finance	X	X	X	X	X	X	X	X
Public Utility	X	X	X	X	X	X	X	X
Municipal and Government	X	X	X	X	X	X	X	X
Handbook of Common Stock		X			X	X	X	X
Dividend Record		X			X	X		X
Fairchild's Financial Manual of Retail Stores	X	X	X	X	X	X	X	X
Wiesenberger Investment Company Service	X	X	X	X	X	X	X	X
Handbook of Labor Statistics (current edition)	X	X						

Government documents and statistical sources	Industrial/organization overview	Individual company/ organization	Historical	Biographical	Current financial	Past financial	Projected financial	Comparative financial
American Statistics Index Annual Supplementary Index	X							X
Survey of Current Business	X							X
Productivity Index for Selected Industries (current edition)	X							X
Annual Survey of Manufacturers Value of Produce Shipments (current edition)	X					X		
Directories								
F & S Index of Corporate Change	X	X			X	X	X	X
Director of Corporate Affiliates Plus Geographical Index		X						
The Corporate Finance Sourcebook, 1980 (lists Fortune 500 companies)		X		X				
Greenwood Encyclopedia of American Institutions Labor Unions	X			X				
Bibliographical Dictionary of American Labor Leaders				X				
Dictionary of Labor Biography				X				
American Labor Sourcebook	X	X	X	X				

Prentice-Hall provides:

1. *Labor Relations Guide*, which contains two volumes. Volume I covers employee relations guides, fair employment practices, cost-of-living index, wages and hours, equal-pay law, labor relations, state labor laws, reemployment of veterans, and occupational safety and health bargaining with unions. Volume II covers federal laws and orders, wage-hour regulations and interpretations, and other federal rules and regulations.

2. *Personnel Management and Industrial Relations*, which contains sections on bargaining, clause checklist and solution finder, union contracts, clauses and analyses, union security and representation, grievances, arbitration, and strikes.

3. *Public Personnel Administration*, which contains three volumes. Volume I, "Labor-Management Relations," covers public-sector bargaining problems, such as union contract clauses and grievance procedures. Volumes II and III, "Public Employment Relations Law," contain a listing of public employment labor and management relations laws, regulations by state, and state laws and regulations pertaining to public employee bargaining.

Bureau of National Affairs provides:

1. *Labor Management Relations*, which covers the full text of federal and state court decisions, including summaries of National Labor Relations Board cases.

2. *Fair Employment Practices*, which is a comprehensive guide to equal employment opportunity laws, fair employment practice policies, and affirmative action programs.

3. *Wage and Hour Guide*, which is a guide to the text and court decisions in wage/hour cases since ratification of the Fair Labor Standards Act (FLSA) in 1938. It includes all federal laws, rules, regulations, interpretations, enforcement procedures, and administrative decisions of the Walsh-Healey Act. Detailed coverage includes child labor, operative pay, recordkeeping, public contracts, litigation, administration and exemptions, and FLSA coverage.

The sources these companies offer are included in various sections of this book. One of the greatest advantages in utilizing these services is the personal hands-on experience gained in locating appropriate information for contract analysis.

Private consulting companies offer another avenue for obtaining information valuable to the investigator. Both union and management analysts need to gather comparative information. These organizations also offer training programs geared to expanding skills in acquiring information.

Appendix A:

Answers to Skill-Building Exercises

CHAPTER 2

1. Figure current straight-time payroll cost.

    a. Scheduled straight-time work year =
    52 weeks X 40 hrs/week = 2,080 hours/year.

    b. Average rate of pay = $3.00 X 2,080 hours = $6,240/employee for a year

    c. 500 employees X $6,240 = $3,120,000 = total straight-time payroll cost

2. Compute the cost of:

    a. 1 percent wage increase

        1. $3,120,000 payroll X .01 = $31.200

    b. 1¢ wage increase

        1. 2,080 hours/year X 500 employees = 1,040,000 total work hours

        2. 1,040,000 X .01 = $10,400

3. Total productive hours per employee

    a. Each employee works 2,080 hours per scheduled year
    b. Each employee averages 150 overtime hours per year
    c. 2,080 + 150 = 2,230 hours per year

4. Straight-time productive hours for each employee is the scheduled work year minus any paid time off. Paid time includes vacations, holidays, and personal leave time.

    a. 2,080 hours/year is the scheduled work year
    (52 weeks/year X 40 hours/week = 2,080 hours)

b. 10 day vacation
   10 days X 8 hours/day = 80 hours/employee

c. 6 holidays
   6 days X 8 hours/day = 48 hours/employee

d. 2 personal leave days
   2 days X 8 hours/day = 16 hours/employee

   Total = 144 hours/employee

Straight-time productive hours = 2,080 – 144 nonproductive hours
= 1,936 hours

5. What is the cost per hour to the company of:

   a. 10 days vacation for 500 employees?

      1. From 4. above, each employee receives 80 hours/year

      2. 80 hours X 500 employees X \$3.00/hour wage = \$120,000

      3. From question 2., total work hours equals 1,040,000

      4. Cost per hour of 10 days vacation =

$$\frac{\text{Total cost of benefit}}{\text{Total work hours}} = \frac{\$120{,}000}{1{,}040{,}000} = 11.5¢ \text{ per hour}$$

      5. Cost for straight-time productive hours from question 4.
      Straight-time productive hours per employee equals 1,936 hours
      Total straight-time productive hours = 1,936 X 500 = 968,000 hours

$$\frac{\$120{,}000}{968{,}000 \text{ hours}} = 12.3¢ \text{ per hour}$$

      6. Cost for total productive hours from question 3.
      Total productive hours per employee equals 2,230 hours
      Total productive hours = 2,230 X 500 employees = 1,115,000 hours

$$\frac{\$120{,}000}{1{,}115{,}000} = 10.7¢ \text{ per hour}$$

b. Six paid holidays?

1. From 4. above, each employee receives 48 hours/year of holiday time

2. 48 hours X 500 employees X $3.00/hour = $72,000

3. From question 2., total work hours equal 1,040,000

4. Cost per hour of the six paid holidays =

$$\frac{\text{Total cost of benefit}}{\text{Total work hours}} = \frac{\$72{,}000}{1{,}040{,}000} = 6.9¢ \text{ per hour}$$

5. Straight-time productive cost $= \dfrac{\$72{,}000}{968{,}000 \text{ hours}} = 7.4¢$ per hour

6. Total productive hours cost $= \dfrac{\$72{,}000}{1{,}115{,}000} = 6.4¢$ per hour

c. Overtime?

1. From the information in the example, we must assume 100 percent replacement. There is no estimate of added cost for personnel time, benefits, and so forth.

2. Overtime averages 150 hours per employee per year
500 employees X 150 hours = 75,000
75,000 hours X $4.50 overtime wage rate = $337,500

3. Cost of overtime as a benefit for a scheduled work year =

$$\frac{\text{Cost of benefit}}{\text{Total hours worked}} = \frac{\$337{,}500}{1{,}040{,}000} = 3.2¢ \text{ per hour}$$

4. Cost for straight-time productive hours = $337,500
1,936 hours (from question 4.) X 500 employees

$$\frac{\$337{,}500}{968{,}000 \text{ hours}} = 34.8¢ \text{ per hour}$$

5. Cost for total productive hours $= \dfrac{\text{Total cost of benefit}}{\text{Scheduled hours + overtime}} =$

$$\frac{\$337{,}500}{2{,}230 \times 500} = \frac{\$337{,}500}{1{,}115{,}000} = 30.2¢ \text{ per hour}$$

6. What is the cost of:

   a. 18 percent increase in wages?

      1. From question 1., straight-time payroll cost = \$3,120,000
      2. From question 2a., 1 percent wage increase = \$31,200
      3. 18 percent = \$31,200 × 18 = \$561,600

   b. 80¢ per hour increase in wages?

      1. Total payroll cost = \$3,120,000
      2. From question 2a., 1¢ increase = \$10,400
      3. 80¢ increase = \$10,400 × 80 = \$832,000

7. What is the true cost of a:

   a. 1 percent increase in wages?

      1. From question 5.:

10 days vacation	=	\$120,000	11.5¢/hour
6 paid holidays	=	72,000	6.9¢/hour
overtime	=	337,500	3.2¢/hour
2 personal leave days	=	24,000	2.3¢/hour
Total cost	=	\$553,500	52.7¢

      2. The total cost of the benefits is approximately 18 percent of total payroll cost.

         \$553,500 - \$3,120,000 total payroll = .177

      3. Or, if you divide the cents per hour figure of .527 by the average wage of \$3.00 per hour, you arrive at approximately 18 percent of total.

      4. Add .18 percent to the 1 percent = 1 + .18 = 1.18 percent

      5. To find the true cost of 1 percent figure

         \$3,120,000 × 1.18 = \$36,816

   b. 1¢ increase?

      1. From question 2., total work hours = 1,040,000
      2. 1¢ it is now known includes approximately 18 percent in benefits
      3. 1,040,000 × .0118 = \$12,272 for a true 1¢ increase

CHAPTER 3

1. What is the current straight-time payroll and with overtime added?

   a. Straight time

      1. Scheduled work year = 52 weeks X 40 hours/week = 2,080 hours
      2. Total work hours = 2,080 X 500 = 1,040,000 hours
      3. 1,040,000 hours X $6.00 hour = $6,240,000

   b. With overtime

      1. 150 hours/employee X 500 employees X $9.00 hour = $675,000
      2. $6,240,000 + $675,000 = $6,915,000

2. Vacation benefit cost with replacement ratio and replacement cost factor

   1. 10 days vacation = 10 days X 8 hours day = 80 hours/employee

      a. 74 percent replacement ratio X 250 employees (50 percent assumption under 5 years) = 185 employees

      b. 10 percent replacement cost factor $6.00 X 1.10 = $6.60

      c. 185 employees X $6.00 hour X 80 hours = $97,680

   2. 15 days after 5 years =

      a. 15 days X 8 hours day = 120 hours/employee

      b. 74 percent replacement ratio X 250 employees = 185 replacement employees

      c. 10 percent cost factor = $6.00 hour X 1.10 = $6.60

      d. 185 employees X $6.60 X 120 hours = $146,520

   3. Cost of benefit = $97,680 + $146,520 = $244,200

   4. Cost per hour of benefit $= \dfrac{\$244{,}200}{1{,}040{,}000 \text{ hours}} = 23.4¢$ per hour

2a. What is the cost of the following union demand?

1. 10 days immediate eligibility (here it can be assumed one-half of the 250 eligible employees will be involved); other assumptions will change this answer.

   125 eligible employees will cost one-half of the old demand for 250 employees at 10 days. Remember the 74 percent ratio is still in effect.

   = $48,000

2. 15 days after 2 years. Again, this will cost one-half of previous 15-day eligibility.

   = $73,260

3. 20 days after five years.

   a. 20 days X 8 hours = 160 hours/employee

   b. 250 employees X 74 percent = 185 replacement employees

   c. 10 percent cost factor = $6.00 X 1.10 = $6.60

   d. 185 employees X $6.60 X 160 hours = $195,360

4. Cost of the demand with replacement factor =

   a. $48,800 + $73,260 + $195,360 = $317,420

   b. Cost per hour $= \dfrac{\$317{,}420}{1{,}040{,}000} =$ 30.5¢ per hour

5. Note the demanded change has resulted in an increase of $73,200 or 7¢ per hour.

3. Current cost of the six paid holidays. Assume 100 percent replacement and therefore no cost factor. This is a reasonable assumption since most organizations close down for principal holidays.

   a. 6 days X 8 hours X $6.00 hour X 500 employees = $144,000

   b. What is the cost with three added days?

   9 days X 8 hours X $6.00 hour X 500 employees = $216,000
   an increase of $72,000

4. What is the cost of two days personal leave?

   a. 2 days × 8 hours × \$6.00 × 500 employees = \$48,000

   $$\frac{\$48{,}000}{1{,}040{,}000} = 4.6¢/\text{hour}$$

   b. If two days are added, the cost doubles to \$96,000 and 9.2¢ per hour.

5. What is the cost per hour of current benefits and proposed changes without replacement cost and ratio factors?

   a. The only benefit affected by this question is that of vacations.

      1. Current cost:

         a. 10 days × 8 hours × 250 employees × \$6.00 = \$120,000

         b. 15 days × 8 hours × 250 employees × \$6.00 = \$180,000

         $$\text{Cost per hour} = \frac{\$300{,}000}{1{,}040{,}000 \text{ hours}} = 28.8¢$$

         c. Note: the increase in current cost figure from the replacement cost is \$55,800 or 5.4¢ per hour. The current cost figure is what is used to report benefit levels to employees.

   b. Proposed change without replacement cost ratios and factors.

      1. 10 days × 8 hours × 125 employees × \$6.00 = \$ 60,000
      2. 15 days × 8 hours × 125 employees × \$6.00 = 90,000
      3. 20 days × 8 hours × 250 employees × \$6.00 = 240,000

      Total \$390,000

      4. Total cost of the proposed change is \$390,000. The cost per hour =

      $$\frac{\$390{,}000}{1{,}040{,}000 \text{ hours}} = 37.5¢ \text{ per hour}$$

      5. Note the current cost of the change is \$72,580 more than with replacement and ratio cost factors.

CHAPTER 4

1. Figure the cost of a 30-minute lunch

   a. 500 employees X .5 hours for lunch X \$3.00 hour X 250 workdays = \$187,500 total cost

   1. Cost per hour = $\frac{\text{Total cost of benefit}}{\text{Total hours worked}}$

   $\frac{\$187{,}500}{1{,}040{,}000 \text{ hours}}$ = 18.0¢ per hour

   b. If the union requested a 60-minute lunch period, the cost would double or \$187,500 X 2 = \$375,000 and 36.0¢/hour.

   c. Here it is cautioned to examine other cost factors such as how would the added 30 minutes be made up, that is, by working overtime or is it assumed productivity will increase because of the increased opportunity to rest?

2. Compute the cost of

   a. Two 10-minute breaks per shift

   1. 20 minutes for breaks X 500 employees X 250 work days = 37,500 hours of lost production for breaks.

   2. 37,500 X \$3.00 hour = \$112,500 cost for the benefit
   37,500 X \$4.50 hour = \$168,750 cost at overtime.

   b. Cost of a 5-minute washup

   1/12 hour X 500 X \$3.00 hour X 250 days = \$31,250
   1/12 hour X 500 X \$4.50 overtime X 250 days = \$46,875.

3. The best way currently to figure the cost of these benefits is by using a historical trendline, that is, base the future cost on past experience. To compute the cost per hour is to place total estimated cost over total work hours and divide.

4. Uniform cost

a. Union option for all employees

500 employees X \$100 = \$50,000 total cost

$$\text{Cost per hour} = \frac{\$50{,}000}{1{,}040{,}000} = 4.8¢$$

b. Management option for 20 percent of employees

500 employees X .20 X \$100 = \$10,000

$$\text{Cost per hour} = \frac{\$10{,}000}{1{,}040{,}000} = .9¢$$

5. SUB pay plan cost

a. Plan calls for 7¢ per hour.

b. \$200,000 ceiling

1. 2,080 hours scheduled work for each employee
2. 2,080 X .07 = \$145.60
3. 500 employees X \$145.60 = \$72,800 first year liability

The company liability would extend well into the third year of the contract.

It will affect future contracts to the extent that layoffs will deplete the fund below the agreed ceiling.

6. Severance pay cost

a.

a. 100 workers - 20 years service - 2 terminated =	40 weeks eligibility
b. 300 workers - 15 years service - 5 terminated =	75 weeks
c. 100 workers - 5 years service - 1 terminated =	5 weeks
Total eligibility	120 weeks

1. Convert weeks of eligibility to hours

   120 weeks X 40 hours/week = 4,800 hours

2. 4,800 hours X \$3.00 hour = \$14,400

3. Cost per hour = $\frac{\$14{,}400}{1{,}040{,}000}$ = 1.3¢ per hour

b. to increase the benefit to 1.5 weeks for each year of service

a. 20 years of service - 2 terminated = 60.0 weeks eligible
b. 15 years of service - 5 terminated = 112.5 weeks
c. 5 years of service - 1 terminated = 7.5 weeks

180 weeks

1. Convert weeks of eligibility to hours

   180 weeks X 40 hours/week = 7,200 hours

2. 7,200 hours X \$3.00 hour = \$21,600

3. Cost per hour = $\frac{\$21{,}600}{1{,}040{,}000 \text{ hours}}$ = 2.0¢ per hour

The cost of the proposed change would be \$7,200 or .7¢ per hour additional to management.

Appendix B:

Ratio Definitions and Charts

The source of all the data used in the examples is the U.S. Treasury, Internal Revenue Service. The definitions and significance of ratios and factors are explained below in terms of standard usage.

Net Sales: The IRS's equivalent term, business receipts, is defined as gross operating receipts arising from the principal business activity less allowances, rebates, and returns. These amounts also include rents reported as the principal business income by corporations in manufacturing that frequently rent products rather than sell them, such as automatic data-processing equipment.

Total Receipts: Includes gross taxable receipts and nontaxable interest received from state and local government obligations. Included are business receipts (see Net Sales), interest on government obligations, other interest, rents, royalties, net short-term and long-term capital gains or losses, net gains on noncapital assets, dividends from domestic and foreign corporations, and other receipts.

Cost of Operations: The IRS term, cost of sales and operations, comprises direct costs incurred in providing goods or services, including costs of materials used in manufacturing, cost of goods purchased for resale, direct labor, and any operating expenses not separately identified in the corporation tax return.

Bad Debts: These include bad debts that occurred during the year or a reasonable addition to an allowance or reserve for bad debts. For banks and domestic building and loan associations, corporate or government debt evidenced by certain bonds that became worthless are chargeable as bad debts. For other corporations, such losses are subject to the special capital gain or loss provisions of the law.

Taxes: Taxes paid include the amount reported as ordinary and necessary business deductions as well as identifiable amounts reported as part of the cost of sales and operations. Included among the deductible taxes are ordinary state

---

These ratio definitions for the following charts are as used in the 1980 *Corporation Income Tax Returns Source Book, Statistics of Income.*

and local taxes paid or accrued during the year, Social Security and payroll taxes, unemployment insurance taxes, import and tariff duties, and business, license, and privilege taxes. Income and profits taxes paid to foreign countries or United States possessions are also deductible unless claimed as a credit against income tax. Not deductible are such taxes as federal income and excess profit taxes, gift taxes, taxes assessed against local benefits, and federal taxes paid on interest tax-free covenant bonds.

Interest: Interest paid in connection with business indebtedness is deductible as an ordinary and necessary business expense. Included in the statistics is interest paid on deposits and withdrawable shares by banking and saving institutions. For installment purchases, interest paid includes amounts stated in the contract and certain unstated amounts of interest, as provided in the IRS Code.

Depreciation: A deduction from gross income of a reasonable allowance for the exhaustion, wear and tear, or obsolescence of property used in a trade or business, or of property held for the production of income. The deduction is computed by a number of methods permissible by law.

Depletion: A deduction allowable for the exhaustion of natural deposits or timber. There are two basic types of depletion allowances, cost and percentage, but no distinction between them is made in this publication.

Amortization: This includes the sum of mineral exploration and development expenditures, organizational expenditures, as well as accelerated write-offs in lieu of depreciation for certified pollution control facilities, coal mining safety equipment, railroad rolling stock, railroad grading and tunnel bores, and any deductions remaining for emergency facilities certified by the federal government before 1960.

Net Profit before Federal Income Taxes: These are net profits (net income) after deductions from net sales or total receipts of all expense items and before deduction of federal income tax. Net profits may also reflect certain income from related foreign corporations only constructively received.

Current Ratio: This is the relationship of current assets to current liabilities. It is an indication of the ability of a company to meet its current obligations. Included in the computation are the IRS summaries of cash plus notes and accounts receivable, plus total inventories, plus investment in government obligations, plus other current assets, less reserve for bad debts. Inventories, as shown in the corporation return balance sheet, include such items as raw materials, finished and partially finished goods, merchandise on hand or in transit, and growing crops reported as assets by agricultural concerns. Current liabilities are shown as a combination of the following IRS items: accounts payable, mortgages, notes and bonds payable in less than one year, and other current liabilities.

Quick Ratio: This is the relationship of cash, current receivables, and marketable securities to current liabilities. It indicates a company's ability to discharge its current obligations without the necessity of selling off inventories.

Net Sales to Net Working Capital: This ratio indicates the amount of work in terms of sales performed by each dollar invested in working capital. Net working capital is the difference between assets and current liabilities.

Net Sales to Net Worth: A ratio indicating the rate of turnover of the owner's investment.

Inventory Turnover: This is the cost of sales over average inventory, which indicates age and probable saleability of the inventory or length of the operating cycle. Values are computed for industries in manufacturing, wholesale, and retail trades and are excluded (indicated by a hyphen) for all other industries. When year-to-year changes in the classification of industries prevent the computation of inventory turnover, the hyphen is also inserted.

Total Liabilities to Net Worth: This ratio indicates the degree of dependence on creditors rather than owners in providing funds for operating the business, or, in short, the amount of "trading on the equity." Total liabilities consists of the items noted above in current liabilities, plus IRS items, loans from stockholders, mortgages, notes and bonds payable in one year or more, and other liabilities. Net worth consists of IRS items, capital stock, paid-in or capital surplus, surplus reserves, and earned surplus and undivided profits, less cost of treasury stock.

Current Liabilities to Net Worth: A percentage indicating the extent to which current creditors are covered by owner's investment.

Inventory to Current Assets: This percentage is an indication of the liquidity of the current assets.

Net Income to Net Worth: This is the percentage rate of return received by the owners on their investment.

Retained Earnings to Net Income: This is the percentage of earnings in the business. In certain cases this ratio may also reflect distributions from prior years' earnings or property whose value exceeds current retained earnings, causing a negative ratio, and this is indicated by a minus sign (-) preceding the figure. Distributions to stockholders consist of a corporation's own stock, and of cash and other property, generally reported as part of the analysis of unappropriated retained earnings. Liquidating dividends, when identified, are excluded. In those instances where a corporation reported one total for distribution to stockholders and did not identify this distribution as cash or stock, the total is treated as a distribution to stockholders in cash and property other than in the company's own stock.

Ratios for General Building Contractors
(assets size in thousands of dollars)

Description of item for accounting period 7/80 through 7/81	Total	Under 100	100 to 250	250 to 500	500 to 1,000
Number of organizations	55720	25118	11083	7301	5202
Total receipts ($ million)	82553.1	4354.2	5027.7	6792.9	9555.4
Selected Operating Factors as Percent of Net Sales					
Cost of operations	83.1	70.5	74.5	80.7	82.6
Compensation of officers	2.8	6.0	6.1	4.9	3.4
Repairs	.3	.3	.4	.2	.3
Bad debts	.1	.1	.0	.1	.1
Rent on business property	.3	.6	.5	.4	.3
Taxes (excl. federal tax)	1.3	1.8	1.9	1.4	1.4
Interest	1.2	1.3	1.6	1.3	1.0
Deprec./deplet./amortiz.*	1.1	1.5	1.6	1.2	1.0
Advertising	.2	.2	.3	.1	.2
Pensions and other benef. plans	.7	.4	.5	.7	.6
Other expense	5.3	11.8	8.0	4.9	5.4
Net profit before tax	3.6	5.4	4.5	3.8	3.8
Net inc.	2.8	2.6	2.6	3.0	2.7
Selected Sample Financial Ratios (number of times ratio is equal to one)					
Current ratio	1.3	1.3	1.6	1.4	1.5
Net sales to net wkg. capital	10.8	39.9	11.2	12.6	10.8
Inventory turnover	8.3	35.6	11.1	9.6	9.3
Selected Sample Financial Factors in Percentages					
Current liab. to net worth	2.2	1.5	1.3	1.5	1.5
Inventory to net assets	28.6	19.1	29.4	33.1	31.9

*Depreciations largest factor.

Source: 1980 Corporation Income Tax Returns Source Book, Statistics of Income, Department of Treasury, Internal Revenue Service, Washington, D.C., publication 1053, p. 263.

1,000 to 5,000	5,000 to 10,000	10,000 to 25,000	25,000 to 50,000	50,000 to 100,000	100,000 to 250,000	250,000 and over
5587	522	299	74	–	12	–
25615.3	5792.1	8422.7	3473.2	–	2844.2	–
84.4	84.7	87.7	84.2	–	82.9	–
2.9	2.1	1.3	1.2	–	.7	–
.3	.3	.2	.2	–	.3	–
.1	.2	.1	.1	–	.0	–
.3	.3	.2	.4	–	.3	–
1.3	1.1	1.0	1.1	–	.7	–
1.0	1.3	1.1	1.7	–	1.5	–
.9	.8	.8	1.2	–	1.5	–
.1	.1	.1	.3	–	.2	–
.9	.9	.6	.5	–	1.0	–
4.5	4.4	3.3	5.4	–	6.7	–
3.3	3.6	3.5	3.6	–	4.0	–
2.7	2.9	3.0	3.0	–	2.6	–
1.3	1.4	1.4	1.4	–	1.2	–
11.6	7.4	9.1	6.3	–	15.6	–
9.1	5.8	7.7	5.6	–	15.6	–
2.4	3.8	14.8	2.3	–	1.6	–
27.6	29.4	28.3	28.8	–	15.9	–

Ratios for Bakery Products
(assets size in thousands of dollars)

Description of item for accounting period 7/80 through 7/81	Total	Under 100	100 to 250	250 to 500	500 to 1,000
Number of organizations	3300	1287	289	476	294
Total receipts ($ million)	12221.2	138.2	313.0	473.2	448.7
Selected Operating Factors as Percent of Net Sales					
Cost of operations	61.5	51.5	84.5	67.4	67.0
Compensation of officers	1.6	14.6	4.1	8.5	4.0
Repairs	.9	1.0	.1	1.3	1.2
Bad debts	.1	–	–	.0	.1
Rent on business property	1.1	4.7	.6	2.0	1.2
Taxes (excl. federal tax)	2.8	3.2	1.9	3.2	3.9
Interest	1.0	1.8	.1	1.1	1.4
Deprec./deplet./amortiz.*	2.4	3.7	1.1	2.6	3.0
Advertising	2.2	.5	.2	.5	.2
Pensions and other benef. plans	2.7	2.0	.3	3.5	1.0
Other expense	19.5	21.4	5.9	12.4	16.0
Net profit before tax	4.0	4.9	1.2	2.7	1.1
Selected Sample Financial Ratios (number of times ratio is equal to one)					
Current ratio	1.6	.5	.9	1.1	1.2
Net sales to net wkg. capital	14.8	–	129.2	45.6	27.4
Inventory turnover	9.5	24.3	23.5	20.2	17.0
Selected Sample Financial Factors in Percentages					
Current liab. to net worth	51.0	–	27.0	96.6	135.7
Inventory to net assets	36.4	13.5	44.6	18.8	20.8

*Depreciations largest factor.

Source: 1980 Corporation Income Tax Returns Source Book, Statistics of Income, Department of Treasury, Internal Revenue Service, Washington, D.C., publication 1053, p. 39.

1,000 to 5,000	5,000 to 10,000	10,000 to 25,000	25,000 to 50,000	50,000 to 100,000	100,000 to 250,000	250,000 and over
395	360	28	85	–	5	4
2538.6	882.5	1171.2	627.9	–	1573.4	4001.0
67.6	68.1	61.9	60.4	–	61.8	53.6
2.0	1.3	1.9	.8	–	.3	.5
.8	.7	.9	1.8	–	1.3	.9
.2	.3	.1	.1	–	.1	.1
1.1	.7	1.4	.8	–	.9	1.1
2.9	2.2	2.5	2.9	–	2.4	2.9
.9	.7	1.0	1.0	–	.8	1.2
2.3	2.2	2.5	2.7	–	2.3	2.3
.7	.8	1.2	1.6	–	1.0	4.8
2.3	1.7	3.2	3.1	–	3.5	3.0
16.0	17.7	21.1	20.6	–	21.1	23.2
3.2	3.5	3.0	4.2	–	4.4	6.4
1.8	1.4	1.6	1.6	–	1.7	1.8
13.2	21.3	16.9	15.9	–	13.8	11.2
12.2	15.2	18.1	8.9	–	9.0	5.8
60.2	74.8	61.4	45.5	–	49.5	34.4
32.3	29.0	20.8	42.7	–	39.0	46.3

Ratios for Newspapers
(assets size in thousands of dollars)

Description of item for accounting period 7/80 through 7/81	Total	Under 100	100 to 250	250 to 500	500 to 1,000
Number of organizations	4678	2216	782	516	480
Total receipts ($ million)	22881.7	335.5	255.1	373.7	652.2
Selected Operating Factors as Percent of Net Sales					
Cost of operations	54.7	44.3	65.9	64.5	63.2
Compensation of officers	1.5	11.5	6.9	5.1	4.6
Repairs	.6	.5	.4	.9	1.4
Bad debts	.7	.5	.5	1.0	.5
Rent on business property	.9	2.4	2.4	1.3	.9
Taxes (excl. federal tax)	3.3	3.9	2.2	3.7	3.3
Interest	1.9	1.2	1.3	1.0	1.0
Deprec./deplet./amortiz.*	4.2	1.8	2.3	3.4	3.2
Advertising	.3	.1	.6	.1	.0
Pensions and other benef. plans	2.5	5.1	.2	1.3	1.1
Other expense	17.3	26.9	15.3	15.3	14.0
Net profit before tax	11.8	1.8	1.9	2.4	6.6
Selected Sample Financial Ratios (number of times ratio is equal to one)					
Current ratio	1.5	1.7	1.4	2.0	1.9
Net sales to net wkg. capital	11.5	14.8	18.6	9.3	8.7
Inventory turnover	17.2	99.5	244.2	52.7	30.8
Selected Sample Financial Factors in Percentages					
Current liab. to net worth	37.2	73.3	73.6	56.9	44.0
Inventory to net assets	12.8	2.7	1.5	5.8	8.7

*Depreciations largest factor.

Source: 1980 Corporation Income Tax Returns Source Book, Statistics of Income, Department of Treasury, Internal Revenue Service, Washington, D.C., publication 1053, p. 64.

1,000 to 5,000	5,000 to 10,000	10,000 to 25,000	25,000 to 50,000	50,000 to 100,000	100,000 to 250,000	250,000 and over
474	59	66	25	21	19	15
1385.6	592.2	1340.5	1361.0	1771.4	3710.6	11903.4
58.2	58.3	57.5	58.7	62.4	59.3	49.7
4.2	1.7	1.6	1.2	.9	.8	.8
.8	.8	.7	.7	.6	.5	.6
.6	.9	.7	.5	.6	.6	.7
1.2	.7	.8	.3	.4	.8	1.0
3.2	3.6	3.5	3.1	3.4	3.5	3.2
2.1	2.1	1.8	1.4	2.2	2.2	2.0
3.7	3.9	4.5	3.3	3.8	4.1	4.6
.1	.2	.2	.1	.6	.2	.3
2.0	2.4	2.4	2.0	2.3	2.4	2.9
15.8	17.6	14.3	10.2	9.6	13.5	21.2
7.9	7.6	11.6	18.3	12.9	11.9	12.7
2.1	2.0	1.7	1.7	1.6	1.9	1.2
6.8	6.6	8.9	8.9	8.8	7.5	20.2
19.3	14.7	19.7	18.0	25.8	20.2	13.5
41.5	39.0	32.9	36.1	39.0	24.8	38.7
11.2	13.7	11.5	13.2	8.3	11.0	15.5

Ratios for Ferrous Metal Industries; Miscellaneous Primary Metal Products
(assets size in thousands of dollars)

Description of item for accounting period 7/80 through 7/81	Total	Under 100	100 to 250	250 to 500	500 to 1,000
Number of organizations	2745	890	353	249	379
Total receipts ($ million)	85143.8	56.5	107.4	232.9	629.0
Selected Operating Factors as Percent of Net Sales					
Cost of operations	72.8	43.4	66.2	63.5	65.8
Compensation of officers	.5	20.4	7.0	5.7	6.9
Repairs	5.2	.9	.5	1.5	1.1
Bad debts	.1	.1	.1	–	.2
Rent on business property	.6	4.0	2.3	1.6	1.3
Taxes (excl. federal tax)	2.3	5.9	4.0	2.7	3.7
Interest	2.6	.6	3.7	2.4	2.2
Deprec./deplet./amortiz.*	4.2	3.4	6.0	2.9	3.2
Advertising	.2	–	.5	.1	.1
Pensions and other benef. plans	4.0	.6	4.4	.6	2.8
Other expense	5.3	11.4	10.0	14.8	11.0
Net profit before tax	2.0	9.3	(4.6)	4.1	1.7
Selected Sample Financial Ratios (number of times ratio is equal to one)					
Current ratio	1.6	.8	1.0	.9	1.4
Net sales to net wkg. capital	7.7	–	–	–	12.6
Inventory turnover	6.1	–	17.4	13.3	9.6
Selected Sample Financial Factors in Percentages					
Current liab. to net worth	70.6	–	149.3	47.9	144.2
Inventory to net assets	34.4	.4	21.7	23.4	25.3

*Depreciations largest factor.

Source: 1980 Corporation Income Tax Returns Source Book, Statistics of Income, Department of Treasury, Internal Revenue Service, Washington, D.C., publication 1053, p. 89.

1,000 to 5,000	5,000 to 10,000	10,000 to 25,000	25,000 to 50,000	50,000 to 100,000	100,000 to 250,000	250,000 and over
562	100	86	39	22	23	29
2256.5	1272.5	2203.1	2112.1	2262.4	4803.7	68928.3
72.4	74.4	76.2	76.9	76.7	74.3	72.4
3.2	2.3	1.7	1.0	.6	.5	.2
1.0	1.3	1.2	.8	1.6	2.9	6.0
.2	.1	.3	.1	.1	.2	.1
.5	.3	.4	.5	.5	.5	.6
2.9	2.6	2.2	2.1	2.3	1.9	2.3
1.8	2.2	2.0	1.9	2.6	2.9	2.7
2.8	3.5	2.9	2.9	2.9	2.7	4.5
.2	.2	.2	.2	.1	.2	.3
2.9	1.6	2.0	2.2	3.6	2.9	4.4
7.7	9.3	8.4	7.3	7.0	8.3	4.7
4.2	2.2	2.5	3.9	3.7	2.5	1.8
1.6	1.4	1.6	1.9	1.7	1.8	1.5
9.4	11.8	8.0	6.1	6.4	5.5	7.8
8.4	8.1	5.4	5.0	4.5	3.6	6.4
77.0	96.3	75.6	63.1	79.7	75.7	67.8
31.2	33.0	43.3	44.2	46.3	51.7	32.3

Ratios for Metal Forgings and Stampings
(assets size in thousands of dollars)

Description of item for accounting period 7/80 through 7/81	Total	Under 100	100 to 250	250 to 500	500 to 1,000
Number of organizations	3950	1521	353	501	661
Total receipts ($ million)	12377.0	74.1	61.8	378.9	1194.9
Selected Operating Factors as Percent of Net Sales					
Cost of operations	70.2	57.8	48.5	65.9	69.2
Compensation of officers	2.6	10.9	7.5	7.7	5.6
Repairs	1.4	.4	–	.4	.4
Bad debts	.4	.2	–	.2	1.9
Rent on business property	.8	6.5	2.2	1.6	1.3
Taxes (excl. federal tax)	2.6	2.9	2.2	2.7	2.8
Interest	2.0	.2	2.5	1.9	1.3
Deprec./deplet./amortiz.*	2.9	2.4	7.9	3.6	2.2
Advertising	.3	.2	1.2	.2	.2
Pensions and other benef. plans	2.5	.5	.4	.8	2.1
Other expense	10.5	20.7	16.7	9.8	9.4
Net profit before tax	3.7	(2.9)	8.6	5.2	3.5
Selected Sample Financial Ratios (number of times ratio is equal to one)					
Current ratio	1.7	2.0	1.5	1.7	1.8
Net sales to net wkg. capital	7.0	5.4	5.8	8.4	8.5
Inventory turnover	5.3	4.8	3.0	9.1	7.1
Selected Sample Financial Factors in Percentages					
Current liab. to net worth	79.9	52.7	135.9	120.9	83.1
Inventory to net assets	38.4	32.8	31.6	26.2	37.5

*Depreciations largest factor.

Source: 1980 Corporation Income Tax Returns Source Book, Statistics of Income, Department of Treasury, Internal Revenue Service, Washington, D.C., publication 1053, p. 96.

1,000 to 5,000	5,000 to 10,000	10,000 to 25,000	25,000 to 50,000	50,000 to 100,000	100,000 to 250,000	250,000 and over
707	113	56	18	8	3	3
2931.5	1491.7	1475.9	1019.3	903.9	803.6	2003.4
70.5	75.2	72.6	71.1	72.3	75.9	63.2
4.3	2.6	1.7	.9	.7	.6	.4
.6	.5	1.0	1.1	1.6	4.9	2.9
.2	.2	.2	.3	.2	–	.3
.6	.5	.5	.5	.5	.6	1.6
2.8	2.6	2.4	2.3	1.8	1.6	3.0
1.7	1.6	1.8	2.0	2.4	1.2	3.7
2.8	3.1	2.7	2.9	2.0	3.3	3.7
.2	.2	.4	.4	.7	.1	.4
1.8	2.1	2.3	2.4	2.0	1.8	5.0
10.1	9.0	7.9	13.5	10.2	5.6	14.6
4.2	2.2	6.4	2.5	5.6	4.2	1.7
1.8	1.5	1.9	1.8	1.9	1.5	1.5
7.3	9.6	10.7	6.0	5.1	7.7	6.6
6.8	5.4	5.0	6.0	4.3	4.3	3.7
67.0	131.6	63.7	56.5	64.8	82.1	99.3
34.6	44.8	41.9	33.1	42.1	44.9	37.2

Ratios for Motor Vehicles and Equipment Manufacturing
(assets size in thousands of dollars)

Description of item for accounting period 7/80 through 7/81	Total	Under 100	100 to 250	250 to 500	500 to 1,000
Number of organizations	2390	403	277	525	438
Total receipts ($ million)	144549.2	2.0	42.4	613.0	864.5
Selected Operating Factors as Percent of Net Sales					
Cost of operations	137.8	74.8	87.8	74.1	72.6
Compensation of officers	.3	–	.5	6.0	3.9
Repairs	.9	–	–	.3	.5
Bad debts	.4	–	–	.1	.1
Rent on business property	.7	33.8	.5	1.1	1.7
Taxes (excl. federal tax)	2.5	2.3	1.2	1.6	2.0
Interest	5.2	9.0	–	.9	1.1
Deprec./deplet./amortiz.*	4.4	25.5	.3	1.1	1.4
Advertising	.9	–	3.7	.8	.4
Pensions and other benef. plans	5.4	–	.6	1.9	.6
Other expense	8.8	38.2	6.0	10.4	13.3
Net profit before tax	(2.0)	(83.7)	(.6)	1.7	2.4
Selected Sample Financial Ratios (number of times ratio is equal to one)					
Current ratio	1.6	3.7	1.5	2.4	2.2
Net sales to net wkg. capital	4.2	6.3	7.2	7.0	6.1
Inventory turnover	6.1	4.1	5.8	6.6	5.3
Selected Sample Financial Factors in Percentages					
Current liab. to net worth	137.7	–	79.7	65.5	68.0
Inventory to net assets	19.3	84.3	36.7	47.3	45.7

*Depreciations largest factor.

Source: 1980 Corporation Income Tax Returns Source Book, Statistics of Income, Department of Treasury, Internal Revenue Service, Washington, D.C., publication 1053, p. 113.

1,000 to 5,000	5,000 to 10,000	10,000 to 25,000	25,000 to 50,000	50,000 to 100,000	100,000 to 250,000	250,000 and over
455	125	74	30	15	13	24
2061.7	1615.8	1813.7	1651.6	1702.2	2543.7	129784.9
74.6	71.5	77.1	71.4	71.7	68.4	72.4
3.3	2.1	1.7	1.2	.8	.8	.1
.3	.5	.6	.6	1.4	1.8	.9
.3	.3	.3	.2	.3	.2	.4
.7	.4	.5	.6	.8	1.0	.6
2.3	2.7	2.4	2.2	2.7	2.8	2.5
2.0	1.4	2.5	2.3	2.5	3.0	5.6
1.5	2.1	2.2	2.6	2.8	2.9	4.7
.5	.4	.6	.4	.5	.7	.9
1.3	2.0	1.7	2.0	3.3	2.8	5.8
10.1	12.2	10.7	8.5	10.4	12.7	8.7
3.2	4.3	2.7	2.1	2.7	2.9	2.5
1.7	2.0	1.9	2.1	2.2	1.6	1.6
6.8	5.7	5.0	4.6	5.2	6.6	4.1
4.6	4.9	3.7	3.7	4.3	3.4	6.3
99.4	63.6	75.9	63.2	55.9	68.8	144.2
47.9	41.9	47.3	49.7	48.1	49.1	17.7

Ratios for General Merchandise Stores
(assets size in thousands of dollars)

Description of item for accounting period 7/80 through 7/81	Total	Under 100	100 to 250	250 to 500	500 to 1,000
Number of organizations	9655	4340	2606	1097	616
Total receipts ($ million)	128405.0	657.2	1321.3	1067.3	994.8
Selected Operating Factors as Percent of Net Sales					
Cost of operations	62.2	72.7	67.7	69.4	72.2
Compensation of officers	.4	3.4	4.9	4.2	1.9
Repairs	.5	.3	.3	.2	.2
Bad debts	.4	.1	–	–	.1
Rent on business property	2.4	4.0	4.4	2.7	1.7
Taxes (excl. federal tax)	2.3	1.6	2.2	1.8	1.8
Interest	3.5	.4	.7	1.6	1.2
Deprec./deplet./amortiz.*	1.7	1.1	.6	.6	.8
Advertising	2.6	1.5	1.6	1.5	1.6
Pensions and other benef. plans	1.0	.2	.2	.9	.6
Other expense	20.7	13.0	14.4	16.5	15.9
Net profit before tax	2.2	1.7	3.0	.5	2.0
Selected Sample Financial Ratios (number of times ratio is equal to one)					
Current ratio	1.3	3.3	2.4	1.7	2.5
Net sales to net wkg. capital	9.7	5.9	5.9	9.2	5.0
Inventory turnover	4.3	4.2	3.6	3.3	2.8
Selected Sample Financial Factors in Percentages					
Current liab. to net worth	136.4	166.7	83.7	142.2	60.8
Inventory to net assets	22.4	71.3	65.4	83.1	77.8

*Depreciations largest factor.

Source: 1980 Corporation Income Tax Returns Source Book, Statistics of Income, Department of Treasury, Internal Revenue Service, Washington, D.C., publication 1053, p. 166.

1,000 to 5,000	5,000 to 10,000	10,000 to 25,000	25,000 to 50,000	50,000 to 100,000	100,000 to 250,000	250,000 and over
622	133	88	41	28	22	31
3628.4	1835.9	3076.7	3017.5	3940.1	5911.4	101782.8
68.1	61.5	66.0	64.3	65.5	64.2	61.1
2.1	1.1	.9	.6	.4	.4	.1
.3	.5	.5	.6	.4	.5	.5
.2	.3	.2	.2	.2	1.3	.4
2.4	2.8	2.5	3.0	2.8	2.6	2.4
2.0	2.1	1.9	2.1	1.9	2.3	2.4
1.4	1.6	1.9	1.7	1.4	2.1	4.0
1.1	1.5	1.2	1.4	1.3	1.6	1.8
2.2	2.8	2.4	2.9	2.4	2.8	2.6
.7	.8	.7	.6	.6	.7	1.1
18.3	22.5	19.1	20.8	20.1	21.5	2.1
1.1	2.4	2.5	1.8	2.0	.1	2.4
2.0	2.4	2.0	2.2	2.0	.9	1.2
7.2	4.7	3.8	5.7	6.3	(38.8)	11.1
4.0	3.2	4.2	3.7	3.7	3.4	4.5
86.1	55.9	76.4	62.1	75.4	109.1	146.9
62.7	53.9	53.1	57.1	56.8	108.5	31.0

Ratios for Trucking and Warehousing
(assets size in thousands of dollars)

Description of item for accounting period 7/80 through 7/81	Total	Under 100	100 to 250	250 to 500	500 to 1,000
Number of organizations	44293	22139	9701	5367	2560
Total receipts ($ million)	61823.1	2621.5	4408.4	4833.4	4409.5
Selected Operating Factors as Percent of Net Sales					
Cost of operations	63.2	65.4	57.5	60.6	67.1
Compensation of officers	2.2	5.8	4.7	6.2	3.3
Repairs	.2	.1	.7	.1	.4
Bad debts	.2	–	.1	.3	.3
Rent on business property	3.3	2.8	2.3	3.4	1.9
Taxes (excl. federal tax)	4.2	3.2	4.4	4.1	3.7
Interest	2.6	1.1	1.6	2.2	1.7
Deprec./deplet./amortiz.*	5.0	4.1	5.0	5.6	4.1
Advertising	.3	.9	.3	.4	.2
Pensions and other benef. plans	2.8	.2	.9	1.3	2.3
Other expense	14.6	16.6	21.8	14.9	13.6
Net profit before tax	1.9	–	.7	.9	1.6
Selected Sample Financial Ratios (number of times ratio is equal to one)					
Current ratio	1.1	.9	1.1	1.0	1.2
Net sales to net wkg. capital	49.7	–	62.2	–	34.3
Inventory turnover	44.6	–	–	–	66.9
Selected Sample Financial Factors in Percentages					
Current liab. to net worth	88.4	–	108.1	106.5	103.8
Inventory to net assets	7.3	3.4	2.2	2.3	6.1

*Depreciations largest factor.

Source: 1980 Corporation Income Tax Returns Source Book, Statistics of Income, Department of Treasury, Internal Revenue Service, Washington, D.C., publication 1053, p. 127.

1,000 to 5,000	5,000 to 10,000	10,000 to 25,000	25,000 to 50,000	50,000 to 100,000	100,000 to 250,000	250,000 and over
3019	291	179	44	31	15	8
12118.9	4146.5	5368.4	3255.9	4539.2	3693.6	11940.9
61.4	64.1	65.5	55.7	72.3	66.8	61.4
2.7	1.4	1.1	.7	.6	.4	.3
.1	–	.1	.3	–	.1	.2
.2	.2	.2	.4	.4	.2	.2
4.1	3.9	5.1	8.8	2.0	2.4	1.9
4.3	4.5	4.1	4.4	3.5	4.6	4.3
2.1	2.0	2.2	3.0	2.4	3.1	2.8
5.0	4.9	4.9	4.2	4.1	5.0	6.0
.1	.1	.1	.1	.2	.2	.2
2.1	2.3	2.8	3.0	3.1	4.1	5.2
15.7	15.3	11.4	19.5	10.5	13.4	12.5
2.2	1.1	2.3	(.2)	.8	(.3)	5.0
1.1	1.0	1.1	1.1	.9	1.1	1.2
75.4	–	–	–	59.7	35.7	17.3
84.1	35.1	62.3	35.4	46.1	21.8	21.6
100.0	109.7	95.5	157.8	109.1	103.0	61.2
4.2	9.9	5.8	9.5	8.2	13.7	8.9

Ratios for Groceries and Related Products
(assets size in thousands of dollars)

Description of item for accounting period 7/80 through 7/81	Total	Under 100	100 to 250	250 to 500	500 to 1,000
Number of organizations	27148	11248	4691	4210	2749
Total receipts ($ million)	162311.3	4240.3	5566.6	9689.7	10956.5
Selected Operating Factors as Percent of Net Sales					
Cost of operations	87.0	72.1	83.1	82.4	85.3
Compensation of officers	.9	5.1	3.6	2.8	1.6
Repairs	.3	.4	.1	.3	.3
Bad debts	.2	.2	.1	.4	.2
Rent on business property	.5	1.6	.6	.8	.6
Taxes (excl. federal tax)	.7	1.2	.8	.8	.9
Interest	.6	.4	.3	.3	.6
Deprec./deplet./amortiz.*	.6	1.0	.7	.7	.6
Advertising	.4	.3	.2	.1	.2
Pensions and other benef. plans	.4	.4	.4	.6	.5
Other expense	7.4	17.0	8.7	10.0	8.6
Net profit before tax	1.0	.3	1.2	.8	.5
Selected Sample Financial Ratios (number of times ratio is equal to one)					
Current ratio	1.4	1.3	1.3	1.7	1.4
Net sales to net wkg. capital	27.1	63.3	61.5	22.4	28.1
Inventory turnover	17.7	62.8	32.6	29.4	21.2
Selected Sample Financial Factors in Percentages					
Current liab. to net worth	142.9	140.2	72.2	102.0	176.1
Inventory to net assets	38.0	17.3	37.2	25.9	33.0

*Depreciations largest factor.

Source: 1980 Corporation Income Tax Returns Source Book, Statistics of Income, Department of Treasury, Internal Revenue Service, Washington, D.C., publication 1053, p. 142.

1,000 to 5,000	5,000 to 10,000	10,000 to 25,000	25,000 to 50,000	50,000 to 100,000	100,000 to 250,000	250,000 and over
3081	329	196	56	28	25	10
39671.2	11846.7	15220.4	10443.6	13678.3	18078.4	22387.0
88.2	87.8	89.0	88.3	90.0	88.4	86.0
1.0	.7	.3	.2	.3	.2	.2
.3	.2	.3	.2	.3	.3	.2
.2	.2	.1	.2	–	.1	.3
.4	.3	.4	.4	.4	.5	.8
.6	.6	.5	.6	.5	.6	.7
.5	.7	.6	.6	.6	.8	1.0
.5	.5	.5	.6	.5	.6	.7
.1	.3	.2	.2	.3	.5	1.2
.4	.4	.4	.4	.4	.5	.4
6.8	7.2	6.5	7.1	6.3	7.2	6.6
1.0	1.1	1.1	1.2	.3	.6	1.8
1.5	1.5	1.4	1.4	1.3	1.4	1.2
24.1	21.1	25.7	28.2	43.1	27.3	31.8
21.0	15.2	16.0	16.6	17.5	14.0	13.1
68.4	151.9	163.5	157.7	233.5	174.7	116.8
34.0	39.7	41.1	42.6	50.0	51.0	35.6

Appendix C:

Additional Resources

CHAPTER 1

Cosmetatos, G. P., and Eilon, S. "Models for Use in Negotiations on Pay and Working Conditions," *Journal of the Operational Research Society*, July 1981, pp. 587-97.
Discusses methodology for developing models to be used in negotiations. Used to provide a rational framework for better understanding of likely consequences of placing or meeting demands and/or assessing offers and conditions under which negotiators can increase individual payoffs. Very mathematical orientation.

Dohrmann, S. "Bargaining '82: Staying Afloat," *American Federationist*, March 1982, pp. 6-15.
Discusses the pros and cons of multiyear contracts. Unions now want dental plans, prescription drug programs, health insurance to cover sickness as well as accidents; and protection against plant closings, relocations, and anti-union employees.

Granof, Michael H. "How to Cost Your Labor Contract," *Bureau of National Affairs, Inc.*, 1973.
Excellent reference book.

Hazelton, W. A. "How to Cost Labor Settlements," *Management Accounting*, May 1979, pp. 19-23.
Gives methods for standardizing computation of benefit costs, providing a vehicle for meaningful benefit cost analysis to be conducted by management. Covers the total cost concept, total cost per hour, and gives examples of how to cost. Discusses costing of holiday pay, specific labor demands, a general wage increase, and what effects these will have on Social Security and workmen's compensation. Includes tables showing calculations of total cost per employee. Has a costing example for health care. Chart on p. 22 gives a breakdown of wages and benefit costs.

Heisel, W. D., and Skinner, Gordon S. *Costing Union Demands*, Chicago: International Personnel Management Association, 1976.
Gives detailed illustrations and models that can be used to do costing in all areas of a union contract.

Kline, S. M., and Maher, J. R. "Educational Level and Satisfaction with Pay," *Personnel Psychology*, 1966, pp. 195-208.

Discusses how we are going to handle the more educated employees and their job satisfaction. Sample shows that higher education is associated with relative dissatisfaction with pay. A potentially exposed work force represents a comparatively less satisfied group than its non-college educated counterpart. In future we are likely to find that more college graduates will hold jobs similar to those who are not college graduates.

Major Collective Bargaining Settlements.

Quarterly press release.

Poster, I. "Collective Bargaining: Warnings for the Novice Negotiator," *Personnel Journal*, March 1981, pp. 203-7.

Cautions to be aware of what is going on behind the scenes and to go slowly at first. Good general article on what to expect. Gives various scenarios so you will know what is going on should something similar happen to you.

Stybel, L. J., "Negotiating Your Own Severance Arrangements," *Business Horizons*, January-February 1982, pp. 77-80.

Table showing salary continuation plans for 108 companies. Talks about base salary/bonus mix, noncash compensation, corporate references, outplacement services and what they provide.

Swidinsky, R. "Bargaining Power Under Compulsory Unionism," *Industrial Relations*, Winter 1982, pp. 62-72.

Results of wage change model show that union security arrangements such as closed shop, union shop, and modified union shop have not had a significant effect on wage settlements during negotiation. A strike tends to increase the size of negotiated wage settlements, plant-level, and local employers' association bargaining units tend to negotiate large settlements, and unions in weakly organized industries are able to extract higher wage settlements than unions in stronger organized industries. This last fact contradicts previous findings and widely held opinions.

U.S. Department of Labor. *Characteristics of Major Collective Bargaining Agreements, January 1, 1980.*

Primarily statistical data. Lists and analyzes 1,550 agreements for firms that have 1,000 workers or more. See charts (pp. 2-8) comparing 1956-80 for duration of agreements, union security provisions, checkoff provisions, total paid holiday time, vacation allowances, severance pay plans, and so forth. Information is provided on an annual basis.

——*Collective Bargaining Agreement for American Federation of Government Employees.*
Refers to public sector bargaining. Covers all contract provisions possible. Reviews the merit system, pay, dues, withholding, employee rights, and appears to be very thorough.

——*Major Collective Bargaining Agreements: Plant Movement, Interplant Transfer, & Relocation Allowances*, July 1981.
Provides information on topics in bargaining. Gives written examples of how contract can be worded for these topics, then shows comparisons of provisions among companies.

——*Major Collective Bargaining Agreements: Wage Administration Provisions*, 84 pages, 1978.
Displays the results of an examination of 1,711 major collective bargaining agreements in the United States. Examines the type of compensation, basic wage structure, wage reopeners, progression, red-circle rates, and so forth. Contains selected clauses to illustrate how negotiators handled either typical or specific situations.

CHAPTER 2

"Caps off COLA?" *Purchasing*, May 9, 1979, p. 46.
5.6 million workers or nearly 60 percent of all union members are covered by COLA provisions. Contracts with COLA expiring in 1979 will be guaranteeing wage increases that average 1.1 percent more than contracts without COLA. Some 1.3 million workers have COLA caps. Union leaders feel "COLA clauses are best method to protect real wages under multiyear contracts."

Cascio, Wayne F. *Costing Human Resources, the Financial Impact of Behavior in Organizations*, Boston: Kent Publishing, 1982.
Chapter Six provides another source to examine costing techniques. This is perhaps the most recent publication in the area. Other chapters focus on behavioral cost to organizations.

Chazen, C. "Compensation Plans: Bottom Line Results," *Management Review*, November 1975, pp. 19-25.
Compensation is payable in cash or property other than stock usually has an effect on earnings/share. The effects of stock options on company earnings are discussed.

"Correct Way to Calculate Roll-Up," *Personnel*, September-October 1980, pp. 44-45.
Gives formula to calculate roll-up. Defines roll-up benefits and gives a case to follow.

"COWPS May Rewrite the COLA Formula," *Business Week*, August 20, 1979, pp. 20-21.
Council on Wage and Price Stability (COWPS). In past, COLAs have acted like automatic raises. These increases of COLA drive up the pay rates in the COLA industry as well as related industry and will keep inflation rising.

Deitsch, C. R., and Dilts, D. A. "COLA Clause: An Employer Bargaining Weapon?" *Personnel Journal*, March 1982, pp. 220-23.
Talks about the most common COLA formula and the number of contracts it appears in. What is COLA? Why do employers oppose it and unions demand it? What is the union's power with COLA?

Duncan, G. J., and Stafford, F. P. "Do Union Members Receive Compensating Wage Differentials?" *American Economic Review*, June 1980, pp. 355-71.
There is evidence that persons joining unions do increase wages at expense of desirable working conditions. There was a regression run on several other independent variables of union status, pp. 1049-55. Article was economically oriented.

Ferguson, E. C. "Wages, Productivity, and the Guidelines," *Economic Record*, June 1971, pp. 217-29.
Shows that wage-price guidelines tend to destabilize rather than stabilize.

"Firms Cut 1982 Salary Increase Estimates," *Pension World*, May 1982, pp. 57-58.

Freeman, R. B., and Medoff, J. L. "Impact of the Percentage Organized in Union and Nonunion Wages," *Review of Economics and Statistics*, November 1981, pp. 561-72.
Survey concluded that percentage organized in a product market has a strong positive association with the wages of union members but not with wages of nonunion members, making union wage differential a positive function of extent of organization. Percentage of workers in a geographic area who are organized appear to raise union wage differential.

Fromm, J. L. "Consider the Hidden Costs of Roll-Up When Calculating Wage Increases," *Business Insurance*, December 10, 1979, pp. 56+.

Greene, R. J. "Issues in Salary Structure Design," *Compensation Review*, 1982, pp. 28-33.
What is correct type of structure for an organization and how much spread should be involved. Gives suggestions of how to compute appropriate and proper range spreads.

Hendricks, W. E., and Kahn, L. M. "Determinants of Bargaining Structure in U.S. Manufacturing Industries," *Industrial and Labor Relations Review*, January 1982, pp. 181-95.
Discusses how a centralized versus decentralized structure can expect bargaining outcomes to be. Gives statistical information about how different variables may affect outcome.

Highton, Frank E. "The Pay Board and Productivity Bargaining," *Personnel*, January-February 1973, pp. 8-20.
Discusses principal uses of and fallacies about the factor of productivity in collective bargaining.

Hyclak, T. "Effect of Unions on Earnings Inequality in Local Labor Markets," *Industrial and Labor Relations Review*, October 1979, pp. 77-84.
Local labor unionization is associated with a more equal earnings distribution across SMSA. Earnings of male workers are more equally distributed in areas with high percentage in manufacturing and less equally distributed in large metropolitan areas and in those with heavier concentration of blacks.

"Include Fringe in Labor Cost Clauses," *Purchasing*, March 11, 1982, p. 47.
There are two ways to establish right indices for labor cost escalators: fashion an index tailor-made from supplier's specific situations; and use Employment Cost Index (BLS, Office of Wages and Industrial Relations, GAO Bldg., 441 G Street N.W., Washington, D.C. 20211, 202-523-1165). Is only two years old and publishes a total compensation index. Index gives percent of change in wages and fringe benefits for six major work groups: nonfarm, nonfarm white collar, nonfarm blue collar, nonfarm serve, nonfarm manufacturing, and nonfarm nonmanufacturing. Also gives percentage of change in wages without fringes for same group.

Kosters, Marvin, et al. *Inflation Control, Productivity, and Collective Bargaining*. New Brunswick, N.J.: Rutgers University, October 18, 1972.
Covers wage controls and what they have done. Discusses productivity past experiences and future and what effect they will have.

Lage, G. M., and Greer, C. R. "Adjusting Salaries for the Effects of Inflation," *Review of Business and Economic Research*, Spring 1981, pp. 1-13.

Discusses across-the-board percentage salary adjustments. Paper gives variations of how this could be done. Talks about behavioral implications, constant percentage increases, salary adjustments to maintain a gap in real or constant dollar terms, and tables showing raise effects with differential rates of inflation.

LeRoy, D. R. "Scheduling Wage Increases and Cost-of-Living Provisions in 1982," *Monthly Labor Review*, January 1982, pp. 16-20.
Tables showing workers who received deferred wage increases in 1982, by major industry group and size of increase, prevalence of COLA clauses in major collective bargaining agreements in October 1981, timing of 1982 COLA review in major contracts, by year of contract expiration and frequency of review. Discusses COLA and deferred wage increases. Gives COLA adjustment formula for 1¢/hour for each .3 rise in CPI. Also discusses COLA caps and indexes.

"Low Productivity: The Real Sin of High Wages," *Engineering News Record*, February 24, 1972, pp. 18-23.
Reports how union practices such as featherbedding lower productivity and often raise unit-labor costs.

Mosier, K. C. "Cost of Living Plan Without Union Label," *Fortune*, July 30, 1979, pp. 115-16.
COLA has added $1.44/hour to labor costs since 1972. Alternatives to COLA based on CPI. Companies, set properly, can keep union out. At Mosier Industries there is a correlation between COLA and productivity. A lot of questions and answers are given about a nonunion company such as Mosier and their COLA plan.

Roscow, Jerome M. "Now Is the Time for Productivity Bargaining," *Harvard Business Review*, January-February 1972, pp. 78-79.
Discusses why United States needs productivity bargaining.

"Scheduled Wage Increases and Escalator Provisions in 1980," *Monthly Labor Review*, January 1980, pp. 9-13.

Sheifer, V. J. "Cost-of-Living Adjustment: Keeping up with Inflation?" *Monthly Labor Review*, June 1979, pp. 14-17.
Chart on p. 14 gives agreement numbers and number of workers covered by COLA, escalator clause only, deferred increase only, reopening only, and five other categories. It talks about industry where COLA is concentrated. Escalator yields trail inflation. Five factors why average COLA less-than-full compensation for inflation.

Stark, Harry F. *Productivity and Bargaining*. New Brunswick, N.J.: Rutgers University, March 1974.
Links between productivity, unit costs, and prices. Relates instances of productivity bargaining.

Steckel, R. G. "Misuse of Roll-Up in Costing Contract Settlements," *Personnel Administrator*, March 1980, pp. 33-34.
Defines what roll-up cost is and what benefits are normally included. Includes a mathematical calculation referring to roll-up benefit.

Stein, Gary. "A Note on Productivity, the Real Wage, and the Accelerationist Hypothesis," *Southern Economic Journal*, April 1975, pp. 683-87.
Accelerationist hypothesis has neglected role of productivity in wage determination.

Suri, G. K., and Pillay, P. S. R. "Productivity Bargaining: A Study of Problems and Possibilities," *Indian Journal of Industrial Relations*, January 1974, pp. 346-62.

U.S. Department of Labor. *Bargaining Calendar of 1982, 11-15, March 1982.*
Discusses COLA.

——*Bargaining Calendar of 1981, 10-15, February 1981.*
Talks about COLA provisions in contracts, COLA caps, adjustment formulas, and deferred increases.

——*Productivity: A Selected, Annotated Bibliography, 1976-78, 1980.*
This references 1,200 books and articles on labor and industrial productivity.

—— *Productivity: A Selected, Annotated Bibliography, 1971-75, 1977.*
Provides information on 1,000 publications referring to productivity.

——*Productivity and the Economy, 1977.*
Pages 38-41–Charts on productivity and unit labor costs and comparisons in manufacturing 1950-67 and 1967-75. Page 29 has a good chart viewing output, unit labor costs, and productivity.

——*Productivity Indexes for Selected Industries, 1978 Edition, 1-10, 1978.*
Contains good chart and graph showing selected industry employment and average annual rate of change in output/employee-hour, found on p. 3. The remainder of the book goes into detail about each selected industry and includes charts, tables, and graphs.

——*Productivity Measures for Selected Industries, 1954-80, 3, April 1982.*
Page 3 gives a chart showing output growth/employee hour comparing 1975 to 1980. Rest of book breaks down into each industry with charts and graphs showing output/employee hour, output, and employee hours.

——*Productivity Measures for Selected Industries, 1954-79, 1-5, April 1981.*
Pages 1-5 is a recap of the 1954-79 productivity comparison. The rest of the book goes into detail about each selected industry and includes charts, tables, and graphs.

——*Wage Calendar, 1977, 13-18, 1977.*
Explains how cost of living increases are calculated, gives number of workers per industry breakdown, and if increases are deferred. Talks about the frequency of review for COLA.

——(Bureau of Labor Statistics). *Major Collective Bargaining Agreements: Wage-Incentive, Production-Standard and Time Study Provisions, 1979.*
Takes various benefit and agreement sections and explains in detail what it is and why it is or is not important. Also shows comparisons of number of contracts with or without certain information.

U.S. Office of Personnel Management. *Performance.*
Prepared by the Workforce Effectiveness and Development Group. Good publication regarding wages, quality circles, and benefits.

CHAPTER 3

Baytos, L. M. "The Employer Benefit Smorgasbord: Its Potential and Limitations," *Compensation Review*, 1970, pp. 16-28.

"Benefits Increase Faster than Pay: Study," *Business Insurance*, December 10, 1979, p. 55.

"Changes in Health Plans Reflect Broader Benefit Coverage," *Monthly Labor Review*, September 1978, pp. 57-59.

Chen, Y. "Growth of Fringe Benefits: Implications for Social Security," *Monthly Labor Review*, November 1981, pp. 3-10.
Employer costs for fringes will increase faster than cash wages at compound rate of .4 percent. Ratio of fringes to total compensation will have risen from 15.8 percent in 1980 to 37.8 percent in 2055. Page 5 chart of actual and projected distribution of cash payroll and fringes for 1950-2055. Page 6

chart shows amount and percentage of distribution of employer costs for fringe benefits by sponsoring sector 1950-1979.

Current Wage Developments: A monthly publication.
Reports on employee compensation, wages, and benefit changes resulting from collective bargaining.

Dalton, D. R., and Perry, J. L. "Absenteeism and the Collective Bargaining Agreement: An Empirical Test," *Academy of Management Journal*, June 1981, pp. 425-31.
Certain provisions in contract make absenteeism easier or more profitable for employees. Absence rates are related to organizational control policies and practices related to absenteeism, at least as enumerated by collective bargaining agreement. Absenteeism is costing U.S. industry $8.5 billion to $20 billion/year.

"Employees Fail to Appreciate Cash Value of Fringe Benefits," *Personnel Management*, August 1979, p. 5.
Too often staff underevaluates fringe packages. They do not translate into dollar terms when reviewing holidays, pension, sick leave. Often these benefits make up one third of an employee's pay. The percentage of companies with staggered work hours and financial assistance for relocation is also cited.

Feldstein, M. S. "Unemployment Insurance: Time for Reform," *Harvard Business Review*, March-April 1975, pp. 51-61.
Page 53 graph shows replacement of wages, loss of net income. Page 54 graph shows distribution of unemployment benefits to households. Benefits are too easy, little incentive for people to return to work. How can we reform situation, how can you improve your experience rating? Introducing individual rating: employee pays for own benefits, then draws from own fund when necessary.

Foegen, J. H. "Basing Benefits on Employee Performance," *Administrative Management*, November 1981, pp. 60-3.
Normally benefits are based on things other than performance. Total compensation is 36.6 percent benefits or $5,560/employee/year. As fringes increase, productivity decreases. Talks about various fringe possibilities. Firms treat benefits as charity rather than pay. Gives examples of benefit plans and their costs to replace current giveaway fringe benefit programs.

——"Is It Time to Clip the Fringes?" *Personnel*, March-April 1972, pp. 36-42.
Wage compensation is becoming ever-larger part of total pay. New benefits

like group car insurance, improvements in working conditions toward satisfaction, feelings, attitudes are increasing. No benefit is cost-free and all benefits are steadily rising. Individual firms and unions need to investigate all long-run ramifications of ever-increasing fringe benefits.

Freeman, J. K., and Luecke, R. W. "Accruing Vacation and Sick Days: The New Accounting for Compensated Absences," *Hospital Financial Management*, July 1981, pp. 56-58.

Freeman, R. B. "Effect of Unionism on Fringe Benefits," *Industrial and Labor Relations Review*, July 1981, pp. 489-509.
Unionism can be expected to raise the fringe share of the compensation package. Page 503 chart of sector and fringe benefits shows comparison for cents/hour spent on fringe, proportion of establishments with fringes. Chart on page 496 is dollars spent/hour on total compensation and on components of compensation, share of dollars spent, production workers in union and nonunion establishments.

Froelich, J. D. "Labor: Union Bargaining Gains Set the Standard for Employee Benefit Packages Everywhere," *Business Insurance*, September 1, 1980, p. 21.
For unions, gone are the days when wages were the only consideration. Unions today want contracts that cover cradle-to-grave needs. Union contracts ensure companies cannot take away collective bargaining that has made tremendous impact on quality and quantity of benefits.

Geisel, J. "Benefits Top $6000 per Worker," *Business Insurance*, December 21, 1981, pp. 3+.
In 1980 employee benefits cost $6,084/employee, up from $5,560 in 1979, which is a 10.3 percent increase. Benefit costs as percentage of total payroll rose to 37.1 percent in 1980. Graph shows employee benefits as percent of payroll, by industry group for 1980.

——"Pension Costs per Employee Grow at Record Pace in 1980," *Business Insurance*, January 18, 1982, p. 22.
In 1980 cost of $1,329/employee for pension as compared to $1,185/employee in 1979, a 12.1 percent increase. Pension costs rise when companies pare their employment rolls.

Hazelton, W. A. "How to Cost Labor Settlements," *Management Accounting*, May 1979, pp. 19-23.
Discusses total cost concept, total cost per hour, and gives mathematical example. Defines hours worked, explains how to cost specific labor demands,

what a wage increase does. A mathematical computation of wages is done. It gives a table of the breakdown for annual total cost/employee, costing of health, inflation, and maturation processes.

Katz, D. M. "Employees: New Benefit Choices," *National Underwriter Life and Health Insurance Edition*, January 9, 1982, pp. 3+.

Leigh, D. E. "Effect of Unionism on Workers' Valuation of Future Pension Benefits," *Industrial and Labor Relations Review*, July 1981, pp. 510-21.
Unions do have an important impact in extending the coverage of private pension plans. Unions increase propensity of workers eligible for a pension to state amount of pension income they expect to receive at normal retirement age. Page 513 has a chart on pension coverage and income for union and nonunion worker.

Levy, J. E., and Mamorsky, J. D. "Conducting an Operational Review of Employee Benefit Plans," *Pension World*, December 1981, pp. 39-41.
Review to determine if corporation benefit plans are being administered in an operationally sound manner, are cost efficient, and are in compliance with federal and state laws. Suggests more preretirement counseling be done and tells what to look for in evaluating company plans.

Lewis, R. F. "Investment in Flexible Benefits Plan Yields High Return in Productivity," *Business Insurance*, October 1, 1979, p. 33.

Lindsey, F. D. "Employee Benefits' Bigger Bite," *Nation's Business*, December 1981, pp. 75-76.
In 1979 employers spent $390 billion, in 1980 $435 billion, and in 1981 $480 billion on employee benefits. Benefit costs rose 197 percent from 1969 to 1980. Benefit payments $117/week/employee in 1980. In 1969 it was $39.46/employee/week. Survey conducted showing 25 main benefits and how they vary in cost from industry to industry and from company to company. A chart of weekly employee benefits/employee 1969-80 and percentage change. Another chart of weekly employee benefit costs by industry in 1980 for manufacturing and nonmanufacturing. A 36-page report on benefits can be purchased for $8 from the Chamber of Commerce of the United States, 1615 H Street N.W., Washington, D.C. 20062.

McIntyre, K. J. "Consultant Predicts Benefit Trends," *Business Insurance*, October 5, 1981, pp. 1+.

Post, E. T. "Get Workers Into the Act if Entitlements Hobble Productivity," *Iron Age*, June 22, 1981, pp. 79-82.

Because of international competition, Americans cannot continue to demand more from work while producing less. Fringe benefits are over 14 percent of total labor costs for organizational workers. Chart on p. 80 compares 1975-80 output/hour of all persons, hourly compensation, and unit labor costs. Employee options to prevent layoffs are outlined in detail.

"Recently Negotiated Pacts Contain Health Concessions," *Business Insurance*, January 18, 1982, pp. 1+.

"Same Condition," *Compensation Review*, 1979, pp. 43-46.
Suggested that vacation accrual not be allowed. Is very difficult to account for on books of company.

Sherwood, S. "Flexible Benefits Can Reduce Costs Over the Long Term," *Business Insurance*, December 14, 1981, pp. 22+.
Flexible benefit plans may cost more to set up, but in end may save money. In some cases, benefit plans shrink things employees do not want. Another option is if employees want more coverage with one benefit, they can opt for a salary cut to help pay for it. Some of the responsibility for benefits goes back to the employee and employee helps to pay for rising costs.

Small Business Administration. *Institute of Life Insurance, New York, March 1975.*
Tells how to set up a business life insurance plan for a sole proprietorship, a partnership, or a corporation. Explains the purposes of insurance coverage.

The American Economy: Employment, Productivity and Inflation in the Eighties, 62, 1980.
Explains why we must not let wages grow with inflation. We need wage-price guidelines.

U.S. Civil Service Commission. *Sick-Leave in United States, 1979.*
Used in public sector bargaining.

U.S. Department of Health and Human Services. *Cost-Control, Health Planning, Medical Care, Cost of, 1980.*
Gives an analysis of cost increases, importance of promoting prevention strategies, and general information regarding health services.

U.S. Department of Labor. *Know Your Pension Plan, 1979.*
A 16-page booklet covering pension plan eligibility, contributions checklist for vesting, and types of benefits.

——, Bureau of Labor Statistics. *Digest of Health and Insurance Plans, 1977–79.* Contains about 140 different company health and insurance plans in detail. Good reference to see how you as a company compare to other companies in same industry. Outlined by company name. Includes life insurance information, retirement, accidental death and dismemberment, sick leave, LTD, and unemployment information.

——, Bureau of Labor Statistics. *Digest of Selected Pension Plans, May 1979.* Digest of 100 selected pension plans under collective bargaining.

Zippo, M. "Employee Benefit Plans in the 1980s," *Personnel*, January 1980, pp. 66–70.
With restructuring of Social Security and ERISA, will these costs keep benefits from rising? Most employers responded they will raise benefits in 1980 or maintain same level. Expected increases to be in dental, legal, and vision care, along with pension benefits, preretirement planning, and time-off benefits. More employees are looking at flexible cafeteria plans, health care, and are trying to cut costs. Alternatives to hospital care are also discussed.

CHAPTER 4

Stybel, L. J. "Negotiating Your Own Severance Arrangements," *Business Horizon*, January–February 1982, pp. 77–80.
Table showing salary continuation plans for 108 companies. Talks about base salary/bonus mix, noncash compensation, corporate references, outplacement services and what they provide.

U.S. Department of Labor, *Major Collective Bargaining Agreements: Employer Pay and Leave for Union Business, October, 1980.*
Outlines the above topics in detail. Gives written examples of how contracts could be worded to be successful and clear. Shows comparisons of provisions among companies.

——*Major Collective Bargaining Agreements: Union Security and Dues Checkoff Provisions, May 1982.*
Examines 1,327 private industry agreements. Discusses dues collection, union activity on company time, and union security.

Bibliography

Anderson, Howard J. (ed.). *Primer of Labor Relations*, 20th ed. Washington, D.C.: Bureau of National Affairs, 1975, p. 50.

Basic Patterns in Union Contracts, 10th ed. Washington, D.C.: Bureau of National Affairs, 1983.

Belcher, D. W. *Compensation Administration*. Englewood Cliffs, N.J.: Prentice-Hall, 1974, pp. 350-53.

Bennett, Amanda. "GM Cuts in White-Collar Pay and Benefits Are Deep, But Workers Don't Seem to Mind," *Wall Street Journal*, April 20, 1982, p. 33.

Brigham, Eugene, and James Pappas. *Managerial Economics*. Hinsdale, Ill.: Dryden Press, 1972, p. 393.

Bureau of Labor Statistics. *Characteristics of Major Collective Bargaining Agreements, January 1, 1980*. Washington, D.C.: U.S. Bureau of Labor, Bulletin 2095, pp. 83, 92-96.

——*Comparative Growth in Manufacturing Productivity and Labor Costs in Selected Industrialized Countries*. Washington, D.C.: U.S. Department of Labor, Bulletin 1958, 1977, pp. 20, 30.

——*Manufacturing Productivity Rates*. Washington, D.C.: U.S. Department of Labor, July 9, 1979.

——*Productivity Indexes for Selected Industries 1977 Edition*. Washington, D.C.: U.S. Department of Labor, Bulletin 1983, 1977.

——*Productivity Measures for Selected Industries, 1954-80*. Washington, D.C.: U.S. Department of Labor, Bulletin 2128, April 1982, p. 2.

Bureau of National Affairs. *Basic Patterns in Union Contracts*, 10th ed. Washington, D.C.: BNA, 1983, pp. 3, 4, 99, 100.

Caples, William G. "The Computer's Use and Potential in Bargaining: A Management View." In *The Impact of Computers on Collective Bargaining*, pp. 79-83, Abraham Segal, ed. Cambridge, Mass.: MIT Press, 1969.

Christenson, Charles, Richard Vancil, and Paul Marshall. *Managerial Economics Text and Cases*, revised 1973; Homewood, Ill.: Irwin, 1975, p. 274.

"Compensation Currents Benefits," *Compensation Review, American Management Association*, Vol. 11, First Quarter 1979, p. 10.

Estenson, David. "Relative Price Variability and Indexed Labor Agreements," *Industrial Relations*, Winter 1981, pp. 71-84.

Ferguson, C. E., and J. P. Gould. *Microeconomic Theory*, 4th ed. Homewood, Ill.: Irwin, 1975, pp. 172, 191.

Finney, H. A., and H. E. Miller. *Principles of Accounting–Intermediate*, 5th ed. Englewood Cliffs, N.J.: Prentice-Hall, p. 472.

Freedman, Audrey. *Managing Labor Relations: Report No. 765*. New York: Conference Board, 1979.

Freeman, Richard L., and James L. Medoff. "The Two Faces of Unionism," *Public Interest*, Fall 1979, pp. 69-93.

Gable, Myron, and Charles Hollon. *A Survey of Current Retail Practices*. New York: National Retail Merchants Association, 1977, p. 74.

Gordon, T., and R. Le Bleu. "Employer Benefits: 1970-1975," *Howard Business Review*, January-February 1970, pp. 93-107.

Granof, Michael. *How to Cost Your Labor Contract*. Washington, D.C.: Bureau of National Affairs, 1973.

Heisel, W. D., and Gordon S. Skinner. *Costing Union Demands*. Milwaukee: Public Employees Relations Library, 1976, pp. 5-10.

Henderson, Richard S. *Compensation Management: Rewarding Performance*. Reston, Va.: Reston Publishing, 1979.

Henle, Peter. "Reverse Collective Bargaining: A Look at Some Union Concession Situations." *Industrial and Labor Relations Review*, Vol. 26, April 1973, p. 565.

Holley, William H., Jr., and Kenneth M. Jennings. *The Labor Relations Process*. Hinsdale, Ill.: Dryden Press, 1980.

Holoviak, Stephen. *Management and Organization Structure in the Coal Industry and Its Effects on Productivity*. West Virginia: West Virginia University Organization for Research and Development, 1980.

How to Read a Financial Report. New York: Merrill Lynch, Pierce, Fenner, and Smith, May 1979.

Jones, E. L., and L. Branham. "Bethlehem, Union Collide on Concessions," *Baltimore Sun*, May 1, 1983, pp. E6-7.

Jorgenson, Dale W. "Energy Prices and Productivity Growth." In *Productivity: Prospects for Growth*, p. 35, Jerome Rosow, ed. New York: Van Nostrand, 1981.

Knezevich, Nicholas. "Third Time's a Charm for Steel Concessions Contract," *Pittsburgh Press*, March 2, 1983, pp. E7-8.

Kochan, Thomas. *Collective Bargaining and Industrial Relations*. Homewood, Ill.: Irwin, 1980.

Lewis, H. Gregg. *Unionism and Relative Wages in the United States*. Chicago: University of Chicago Press, 1963.

Lundquist, Eric. "Sugart Robot System Builds Disk Drives," *Mini-Micro Systems*, Vol. 15, June 1982, pp. 193-95.

National Industrial Conference Board. *Computing the Cost of Your Labor Contract*. Washington, D.C.: Bureau of National Affairs, 1973, p. 7.

——*Personnel Administration: Changing Scope and Organization: Report No. 203*. New York: The Board, 1965.

NLRB v. *Truitt Manufacturing Company*. 351 US 149, 1956.

Oswald, Rudy. "Unions and Productivity." In *Productivity: Prospects for Growth*, pp. 98-99, Jerome M. Rosow, ed. New York: Van Nostrand, 1981.

Pillsbury, William F. *The Use of Corporate Financial Statements and Related Data by Organized Labor*. Bloomington, Ind.: Business Report Number 18, November 1954, pp. 39, 49.

Pyle, William, and Kermit Larson. *Financial Accounting*. Homewood, Ill.: Irwin, 1980.

Rees, Albert. "Patterns of Wages, Prices and Productivity," *Wages, Prices, Profits and Productivity*. New York: American Assembly, 1959, p. 23.

Schall, Lawrence D., and Charles W. Haley. *Introduction to Financial Management*. New York: McGraw-Hill, 1977.

Scheifer, Victor J. "Cost of Living Adjustment: Keeping Up with Inflation," *Monthly Labor Review*, June 1979, pp. 14–16.

Troy, Leo. *Almanac of Business and Industrial Financial Ratios*, 1980 edition. Englewood Cliffs, N.J.: Prentice-Hall, 1980, pp. x–xiii, 23, 43, 83, 121, 163, 183, 205, 241, 243, 261, 313.

Twomey, David P. *Labor Law and Legislation*, 6th ed. Cincinnati, Ohio: South-Western University, 1980, p. 209.

U.S. Chamber of Commerce. *1976, Employee Benefits*. Washington, D.C., 1975.

——*Employee Benefits, 1979*. Washington, D.C., 1980.

U.S. Council on Wage and Price Stability. *Report on Productivity*. Washington, D.C.: Executive Office of the President, July 1979.

U.S. President. *Economic Report of the President, 1980*. Washington, D.C.: Government Printing Office, 1980.

Viscusi, W. Kip. "Strategic Behavior and the Impact of Unions on Wage Incentive Plans," *Journal of Labor Research*, Vol. III, No. 1, Winter 1982, p. 10.

"Welding and Robotics: The New World of Robotic Arc Welding," *Iron Age*, 226, March 1983, pp. 3-30.

Weston, J. Fred. *Management Finance*. New York: Holt, Rinehart and Winston, 1962, p. 247.

Whaley, George L. "The Impact of Robotics Technology Upon Human Resource Management." *Personnel Administrator*, September 27, 1982, pp. 61-71.

Wilcox, Kirkland, and Joseph Miguel. *Introduction to Financial Accounting*. New York: Harper and Row, 1980.

Zaliesky, John. "Cost of Having Clauses: Always Playing Catch-Up," *AFL-CIO American Federationist*, August 1980, p. 12.

Index

About the Author

STEPHEN J. HOLOVIAK is Professor of Labor Relations at Shippensburg University of Pennsylvania. In addition, he is Director of the H. R. Frehn Center for Management at the university. Prior to his teaching career, he spent ten years in private industry as a financial executive.

Dr. Holoviak has published widely in the area of labor relations and compensation. His articles have appeared in *Personnel, Akron Business and Economic Review, Performance and Instruction Journal,* and the *American Journal of Small Business.* Dr. Holoviak is also an active consultant in the area of labor relations and compensation administration.

Dr. Holoviak holds a B.S.B.A. from Henderson State University, an M.S.M. from Frostburg State College, and an M.A. and Ph.D. from West Virginia University, Morgantown, West Virginia.